From I to *I Do*

From I to *I Do*

How to MEET, DATE and MARRY your Mr Right

ARNIE SINGER

Citron Publishing, New York

Published by
Citron Publishing
www.citronpublishing.com

Printed in the United States

ISBN 978-0-9830285-1-2

.

Contact the Author at:
arnie.singer@gmail.com
www.itoido.com

To my Ms. Right, without whose unflagging support I would not be able to continue helping others.

And

To all those searching for their Mr. Right.

TABLE OF CONTENTS

SECTION FOUR   NAVIGATING YOUR RELATIONSHIP

INTRODUCTION

When I first started giving dating and relationship advice, my goal was to help men create committed, long term relationships that would lead to marriage. I was the perfect man for the job. I was forty two years old when I finally stood under the wedding canopy with my bride, after almost two decades of field playing and short and longer term relationships, including one (broken) engagement. I understood how single men think, because I was one of them, or at least had been until very recently. I could help men overcome their fears of commitment and all the other things that were keeping them single, and bring them to the gates of matrimonial bliss.

It didn't take me more than a few months to realize that my quest to tame and domesticate the lone wolf male species was doomed to failure. Men don't want advice about how to commit and build lasting relationships. What they do want is someone to teach them how to pick up hot women. While I did pretty well for myself with the ladies in my single days, my goal is not to teach men how to seduce, manipulate, and conquer in the pursuit of constant self gratification and physical pleasure. There are plenty of self proclaimed masters of the pickup game who are eager to provide instruction on the finer points of their manipulative art. I'll let them ply their sinister wares on their own.

My goal is to help singles build committed relationships that lead to marriage. Almost every single woman I worked with over the past few years professed the sincere desire to be part of a long term committed relationship that would eventually lead to marriage. That's the kind of audience I want to spend my time and energy on to help them achieve their objectives. I got to work.

After hundreds of meetings with single women who claimed to want to get married, I realized a few things:

- ♥ Most had unrealistic expectations of who their Mr. Right would be, which prevented them from having meaningful relationships with real potential mates.
- ♥ Most had no idea how to go about finding the kind of man they wanted.
- ♥ Most continued to make the same dating and relationship mistakes over and over.
- ♥ None of them understood the way men really think and operate.

So I decided to create a practical guide to help women successfully navigate the dating and relationship process and empower them with the tools and skills to find and marry their Mr. Right. This book is the cornerstone of that vast project. My website www.itoido.com is where I continue to elaborate and expand upon the ideas and techniques I teach in this book, and where I continuously answer questions on all sorts of dating and relationship issues.

The book is divided into four sections:

Section one is all about what you should do *before* you begin your search for your Mr. Right. I know you've already been searching for years, but imagine this as a fresh start.

Section two is about meeting your Mr. Right.

Section three covers the dating process, from setting up the date to getting exclusive.

Section four helps you navigate your relationship from inception through engagement. It also covers long distance relationships, workplace romances, breaking up, and planning the wedding.

What happens after "I Do" will have to wait until my next book!

*   *   *

Why should you listen to dating and relationship advice from me, a man...and a rabbi!? I'll give you a few reasons.

I'm a man, so I understand the mind of the single man in a way that no woman can. That means I can let you in on what's going on in the mind of the man you're trying to attract or be in a relationship with. I'm like the player from the opposing team who switches sides before the championship game and brings with him all of his former team's strategies and plays and not only hands them to you, but thoroughly explains each one. Lucky you!!

I dated for nearly two decades in New York City before I found my Ms. Right (in Israel — go figure!) just a few years ago, so I totally understand the challenges, frustrations, disappointments, and general ups and downs of the dating scene.

I married my Ms. Right (now Mrs. Right) and am now the father of two little kiddies, so I can actually tell you how to be in a successful long term relationship and how to transition into marriage. A lot of other dating and relationship experts are single. That doesn't necessarily mean they can't give you good advice, but seriously, would you rather get relationship advice from someone who went through the process and succeeded or someone who is still working on it? If your goal is to eventually marry, you need advice from someone who's been there and done that.

I've spent decades studying thousands of years of the accumulated wisdom of the oldest monotheistic religion in history. That doesn't mean I'm necessarily smarter than anyone else. It just means I might have some insights into life and human nature that others don't. While I never interject any religion into my advice, I do stand firmly by certain moral and ethical principles that many people today seem to consider outdated. I'll never condone malicious, dishonest, or unethical behavior. I'll never advise you to have sex outside of a committed relationship (preferably marriage), but I also won't condemn you if you decide to do so.

I'll always give you my honest opinion without any hype or unrealistic promises. I'm not looking to fill a bunch of pages with fluff and nonsense just to say I wrote a book with a lot of pages. My only objective is to help you find your Mr. Right. Every word in this book is there to make that a reality, and for that reason alone. I'll work hard to earn, and deserve, your trust.

I don't have any secrets to share with you that will magically make your dream man appear and fall in love with you. All I can give you is honest and down to earth practical advice to guide you through the steps you need to take to get from decision to marriage. I promise not to pull any punches or say things just to make you feel good. My goal is to help you find, attract, and marry the man whom you will build a successful marriage and family with. I know it's not easy. Finding a life partner is one of the hardest things you'll ever have to do. But millions of women have done it, and you can too. I want to see you succeed more than anything in the world. I can't guarantee results, but I'm confident that my advice will steer you in the right direction.

SECTION ONE

PREPARATION

Chapter One

Decision Time

It is in your moments of decision that your destiny is shaped.

— Tony Robbins

Are you a casual dater or a serious dater? Huh? Let me explain. Daters can be broadly classified as either casual or serious. The objective of a serious dater is to build a committed relationship. The objective of a casual dater is not as clearly defined. It might be to eventually build a relationship, or it might be to enjoy the moment and move on. Neither serious nor casual is better or worse than the other. Each has its time and place. The problem arises when you say you're a serious dater but act like a casual dater.

So what are you, casual or serious?

If you're a casual dater, your primary objective is to satisfy *your* needs. You want someone who'll make *you* feel good and with whom *you* can have fun. You want someone who makes your knees feel weak, your heart pound faster, your eyes see shooting stars at the very image of their countenance...all the time. Your dating objective is to find that person. If you do, you will continue to date them for as long as they continue to make you feel the way you did initially. As soon as they stop, you'll move on to find someone else who will "bring back that loving feeling." There's a whole world of potential "make you feel good" partners out there, so why not keep looking?

The casual dater is not in the business of giving second chances. Anything short of immediate fireworks is a no-go. If you're looking for personal satisfaction then why not continue looking for that perfect satisfier, and possibly have some fun in the process? No use wasting precious dating time on someone who isn't making your spine tingle from the outset.

Lots of singles claim to be serious daters, but are really just casual daters in disguise. They swear that they really truly want to get married, but they continue to reject potential mates because they just didn't feel that spark on their first date (or first glance) or just didn't feel the way they know they should feel when they're with their "true love". They don't need to waste time dating the person to figure anything out. They know from the get go.

I'm not talking about those times when you're so repulsed you can't look at your date without chucking up your lunch. You don't have to go out with them a second time to know you're right. I am talking about the dates which are not so clear cut, where you might not see heavenly light shows, but you also aren't turned off, and many of the fundamental items on your list are present. The casual daters will blow them off without remorse.

If you're a serious dater, you've decided that the most important objective in your life is to find someone whom you can build a family with and love (i.e. give to) and cherish "till death do you part". You obviously need to feel attracted and excited, but you realize that your feelings will transform and evolve with time and that there will be ups and downs in any relationship. So if date number three isn't as exciting as date number one, you're willing to give it more chances because hopefully date number six will be great again. If your partner does or says something really stupid or insensitive, you're willing to give him the benefit of the doubt and see how he acts on the next two dates.

When you're a serious dater, you are not looking for faults and imperfections in your partner. Instead, you are looking for positive reasons to continue dating him to see if he might possibly be the man you could share life with. You're trying hard to find the good in him instead of searching for his slightest flaw. You go into every date committed to doing everything in your power to make things work. You don't want to move on. You don't want to date anyone else if you don't have to.

If you want to be counted among the serious daters, you must decide right here and now to date for relationship potential, not for perfection.

Most women say they are serious daters, and in theory they are. But in practice, they haven't actually made that decision. Building a committed relationship, particularly a marriage, requires making a conscious decision. Unlike your favorite Hollywood love story, it's rarely a clear cut decision accompanied by a bolt of lightning and fireworks. Every relationship has issues, stuff you wish was different. Every person has flaws. You do, and so does your significant other. You can choose to work on those issues and accept those flaws, or you can decide to try and find another relationship and partner without them. If you've decided that you want to be in a committed relationship, you will attempt to make the relationship work, with all its issues and flaws, because you understand that nothing and nobody is perfect. You realize that although the next relationship might not have this particular issue, it will undoubtedly have another. If you haven't made that decision, regardless of how much you say you want to get married, you will bolt. You'll have reasons and facts to back up your decision. It just wasn't right, there were too many problems, it wasn't a perfect fit, I didn't feel what I feel I should be feeling, I want to wait for true love.

I'm not saying you need to stay with someone regardless of the issues that might exist in the relationship. There are issues that are just too big to overlook or workout. You'll have to decide what those *dealbreakers* are for you. But if you've decided that you want to be in a committed relationship ASAP, you will be much more flexible and open to compromise and workouts, and much more forgiving and accepting of non fatal flaws and imperfections. You will focus on the good stuff, on what's right, instead of just looking for what's wrong.

One of the most popular reasons given by women who are not in committed relationships is, "I'm waiting for true love." I can't really argue with that. How can I tell a woman that she is in love, when she feels that she isn't? What I can do is try to present a realistic definition of "true love" that I believe can only be garnered through the benefit of experience.

What is "true love"? Is it that feeling that you get when you meet someone for the first time that makes you weak in the knees or seeing shooting stars? No, that's chemistry or infatuation. It's not true love.

True love is something that you can't experience outside of a committed relationship. It happens, over time, when you're with someone:

♥ who will appreciate you for who you are, not who they wish you'd be.

♥ who will be there for you when you have to deal with illness, death, unemployment, financial ruin, etc.

♥ who will motivate you to be the best person you can possibly be.

♥ who will lift your spirits, and not smash you down.

♥ who will sacrifice his time and energy, and go out of his way to help you and make you feel good.

♥ who will help you raise a wonderful family.

♥ who will love you when you get old and frail.

♥ who you want to do all of the above for.

The person I'm describing is your soulmate, your *Bashert*, your true love. How do you know when you've found that special person? You don't. You can't.

You see, there's no way you can know if someone fits all the criteria I enumerated without spending a lifetime with them. Sure, if you date someone for long enough you might experience some of those things, like illness, death of a loved one, and unemployment. But you definitely won't see them all, and even the ones you will see might not give you an accurate picture of how that person will act in a marriage with the added stresses of children, and all the expenses and responsibilities that come with them.

When I married my wife I thought I knew everything about her. Then a lot of stuff happened. I moved to Tel Aviv and looked for a job for almost a year. Nine months after our marriage my mother passed away. Then we moved from Tel Aviv to NY to be near my dad. Then we had our first child. Then we moved apartments. Then we had our second child. Then we moved to our first house. And we've only been married for four years! After each of these life changing events I saw new strengths in my wife that I never could have known existed. Our love grew stronger and deeper with each challenge.

There is no way that I could have ever known how she would deal with death until it happened. There is no way I could have foreseen how she would be with two babies, severe lack of sleep, cramped NYC quarters and a dozen other stresses. Would she stand with me in times of trouble, lift me up when my spirits were low, sacrifice her time and energy for me and our children, and love me even when I deserved to be tarred and feathered? I've learned so much about her over the last few years, but there's still so much more I'll learn in the next fifty or sixty. Is the woman I married my soulmate, my true love? I really think so, but I won't be 100% certain until we're both sitting in our rocking chairs reminiscing about our long and happy life together.

Serious daters recognize that true love develops and grows over the lifetime of a relationship. They don't wait for it to magically appear. They try to find a man who has the ingredients and the desire to partner with them to develop it in a committed, long lasting relationship.

So, what kind of dater are you, casual or serious?

Serious daters, continue reading.

Chapter Two

Creating Your I Do List

All our dreams can come true - if we have the courage to pursue them.

— Walt Disney

The first step in your search for your ideal partner is to create a list of criteria that you'd like to find in him. We'll call this your I Do List. You know you've got a laundry list that stretches down the hall and out the front door. I want you to write down every single item in that mental list that you've been carrying around with you since you first started dating. Yes, physically write it down, don't just imagine it in your mind. Seeing your criteria staring at you on a piece of paper (or screen) will make it easier for you to objectively evaluate them.

Be honest. If your only two list items are "nice" and "good heart", you're either not taking this seriously or not being honest with yourself. When I ask someone what she's looking for in her ideal mate and she tells me that all she wants is a nice guy with a good heart, my response is LIAR! You've already dated dozens of

16

nice guys with good hearts, and here you are reading this book. You're looking for more, and that's ok.

Make your I Do List as detailed as possible. For example, if one of your items is "financially secure", be more specific and write down what that means to you. Is there a dollar amount, a particular career path, or maybe just a perception. Getting specific will help you clarify what exactly you're looking for.

Take as much time as you need to create your I Do List. Think about it. Meditate on it. Sleep on it. Dream about it. It's going to be one of your primary guides throughout your search.

Ok, pencils down. Most of you have at least ten items on your I Do List. Some of you have many more. Some of the items on the list are more important to you than others. Some you might be willing to compromise on. Some are dealbreakers. Some of the items on your list might be irrelevant to a happy marriage, and I'll try to tell you what those are and give you some items which I feel you should add instead.

One way to gauge if the items on your I Do List are realistic is to imagine that the man you're aiming for has a male version of the same list. That means the criteria you're looking to find in a man are the same as what he's looking to find in you. If you're looking for someone who is generous, so is he. If you're looking for someone who is in great physical shape, he is too. See where I'm going with this? If you're looking for an All Star, you need to be one yourself.

I'm not trying to discourage you from attempting to find the man of your dreams. I just want you to be sure that your dream is realistic. For example, if you're going after the type of guy who's purpose in life is to date models or women who look like them, unless you're in that category, you're setting yourself up for failure. I know, there are always exceptions, but assume that you're not going to be one of them. If you want to succeed at this game you need to play with the odds, not against them. If you're feeling lucky, buy a lottery ticket.

What about opposites attract? For most men that aphorism relates to career or personality. I know a successful hedge fund manager who will only date teachers and social workers. If you're in law or finance, don't waste your time. Also, it's not uncommon for a type A personality to be attracted only to type B's, and visa versa. But the opposites attract rule doesn't seem to hold true for men when it relates to looks. Even guys who would never be considered the least bit attractive think they deserve a great looking woman. If you've got your sights set on a handsome fellow, realize that he probably wants a woman at his level of attractiveness or higher. Unfortunate, but true. So look in the mirror, be honest, and adjust your sights appropriately.

I'll share a personal story with you. It was my freshman year at college and I had just returned to my dorm room from what I think was my first real date (no, I never dated in high school). I went to speak to my dorm counselor, a wise fellow a few years my senior who I looked up to as a "man of the world". His name was Abe Pikus (Abe, if you're out there, please get in touch! It's been over 20 years). I told Abe about my date, that I had a nice time, but that I wasn't sure if I wanted to go out with her again. "Abe," I said, "she's really nice and I think I like her, but she's just not a 10."

Abe responded with words that I will never forget. "Arnie," he said, "neither are you."

WOW! Abe, you changed my life with those deep, wise words, for which I am forever grateful.

Be honest with who you are, your strengths and weaknesses, your good points and bad. Get your expectations in line with your reality. Now review your list and revise it. Cross out or modify those items that don't jive with your reality. You've just saved yourself lots of heartache, frustration, disappointment, and most importantly, time. You will no longer waste precious time chasing after men who you can tell are looking for something that you're not. That doesn't mean that there's anything wrong with *you*. It has nothing to do with you, it has to do with what's going on in *their* minds and on *their* lists. Don't take it personally. Just stay focused on your revised I Do List and push forward.

We're not done yet. Go through your I Do List again and cross out each item that is irrelevant to building a happy marriage. Let me explain. Many of the qualities that are sought after in a dating partner are irrelevant in a relationship partner or spouse.

Let's take appearance. Physical attraction is an important part of a relationship. But for some of you, looks is at the top of your list. You want a guy who looks good with his shirt off, and feels comfortable in the gym or on the sports field. But you do realize that a guy in his late fifties will look different than he did in his late twenties. Use your imagination. If you've chosen a partner based primarily on his appearance, you're in for a rude awakening down the road, spending the rest of your life with a man who looks nothing like the stud you chose to marry. I'm not saying that physical attraction is not important in a relationship. It is. It just can't be the primary factor in your decision to marry someone.

Another list item common to many, if not most, women is financial stability. Many women focus on the profession or balance sheet of a potential partner. How much is he making now, and how much will he be making in five and ten years?

Making enough money to live comfortably is important. So is having a husband who is around to spend time with you and the kids. Huge paychecks usually come with long hours of work, and sometimes lots of travel. They also come with high levels of constant stress. You need to decide what's more important: a husband who makes more money or has more time and energy to share. It's almost impossible to get both in one man. My advice is to go for a bit less money and a lot more time.

I once pointed out a guy to a woman I was trying to set up. She glanced at him and told me that he didn't have that "zing" she was seeking. After she explained, I understood that she was looking for more of a player. I don't mean someone who'll cheat on her, just someone who looks like a player. You know, a bit mysterious, even dangerous, looking. Someone exciting in an Antonio Banderas type of way. I felt like painting for her the following scene. Imagine being severely sleep deprived with two screaming kiddies both requiring diaper changes and a pot of soup boiling over on the stove. Do you think Mr. Player is the man you want in the room at that moment? Perhaps you'd rather have Sensitive Steve or Reliable Ralph. Think about it. Mystery and challenge is great on a date, but not what you need when the going gets tough.

Here are a few items that I feel you must have on your I Do List:

Kindness

This is vital. You want someone who will always be kind to you and your children. You can tell if a man has this quality from the start by the way he treats not only you but everyone he comes into contact with including waiters, cab drivers, doormen, little kids on the street, and random people he runs across who need a hand. Yes, that includes helping little old ladies cross the street.

Ability to Handle Stress

Life is full of stress. Children are stressful. Finances are stressful. Unemployment, sickness, and death are all stress inducing. A man who can deal with it all will make your life much happier.

Supportive

You want a partner not an adversary. Someone who'll build you up, not knock you down, especially when times get tough. Sometimes the men who are the most driven and successful in their careers are the least likely to support you if you decide to pursue your own career.

Sense of Humor

When your two year old pees all over your new living room carpet, you better have a sense of humor. You don't want a man who'll blow his fuse anytime something goes a bit wrong. He doesn't have to be doing standup at the local comedy club. Just someone who can flow with the punches and not lose his cool.

Someone who shares your basic life goals

You don't have to agree on every detail, but you should be on the same page when it comes to how you plan to raise your children and what value system to practice. For many, this includes religion. It also includes the standard of living you hope to maintain. Someone who dreams of having a Park Avenue penthouse, a home in the Hamptons, and a villa on the Riviera should not marry a social worker dedicated to living and working with an inner city population.

Now let's list some items that I don't consider must haves on your list, but they're things you should at least consider and decide whether they're important to you.

Education

It's not uncommon for college educated women to only want to marry college educated men. Does a college degree make a man a better husband or father? Of course not. Formal education is irrelevant to being a successful relationship partner or parent. But education does play a huge part in the social, intellectual, and cultural interaction that helps form a connection between two people. Many people need a certain level of intellectual stimulation from a partner in order to respect them. For some, intellectual stimulation is more important than sexual attraction, or even sex. So, is education a fundamental, must have, item on your I Do List? No. Is it a valid item for you to have? Absolutely.

Respect

Most women I speak to say that they want a man they can respect. What creates that respect is different for everyone, but the need for it is there across the board. Of course, there are right and wrong reasons for respecting someone. To respect someone just because he has a lot of money is, in my opinion, shallow. To respect someone because he is hard working and determined to succeed is valid. You need to figure out what makes you respect someone, and then decide how relevant it is to your future marital happiness. When you've done that, you can add respect to your list.

Geography

The geographic location you choose to call your home means different things to different people. To some it's simply a place to live, as good as any other on the planet, carrying no emotional attachment. As long as they can maintain the standard of living they've grown accustomed to, they're happy to move somewhere new for a good reason. Others are intensely attached to family, friends, and even to the place itself. I know plenty of New Yorkers who would choose death rather than move anywhere else, especially LA (and NJ, of course). You need to decide how important your place of residence is to you. I think you should never pick location over love, within reason. I can see how moving to Africa from the US might be a deal breaker. But moving from New York to LA? Of course, when there's family involved in the equation, like an elderly or ill parent, the decision becomes much more difficult.

Are you willing to give up love for location? If your answer is yes, you need to include your location as a requirement on your list.

Common Interests

I'll be honest, I'm on the fence about this one. While it's obviously amazing to share common interests with your significant other, my soul tells me it's not a requirement for a happy and successful marriage. Respecting your partner's interests is. My wife and I don't like the same types of movies. She likes cheesy romantic comedies. I can't stand them. I like war films. She hates them. Big deal! Learn to compromise or see movies separately. You'll work it out while you build a beautiful family and share the things that are really important in life. Like a wise man once said, "Don't sweat the small stuff".

Review your list again and get rid of the items that are irrelevant for a happy marriage and add those that are relevant. Your list will probably now be at least half as long as it was when you began. It might hurt to give up some of the things you've been dreaming about for years, but the alternative of being single for another five or ten years will hurt much more.

Wait, you're still not done. If you're really serious about your search and want to get it done ASAP, here's what you need to do. Go through your new, shortened, list and decide which items you will compromise on. Yup, there are items on your list that you'd ideally love to have but are willing to let them go if the other, more important, ones are there. You can keep all of your items as long as you agree that if you have to, you will compromise on these. Now we're getting somewhere.

If you've taken this exercise seriously you should have no more than eight items on your I Do List and be willing to accept five out of eight. You might want to combine some items, like supportive and kind, and make your list even shorter. The shorter your list is, the easier it will be for you to commit to a partner. Just make sure that your short list includes the important items we spoke about. Remember, it's your I Do List, and your future, so only you can modify it.

Now that you've got your I Do List, trust it. There might be times when you are so infatuated with a guy that you'll feel like ditching your list and just diving in. Don't do it. You created your list in sound mind after lots of deep thought and soul searching. You know deep down inside that those list items are things you need to be happy. *Don't ignore your I Do List.* If you feel strongly about modifying it, do so with caution after going through the process we just went through together.

Trust your I Do List. Trust Yourself.

Chapter Three

Preparing for Your Journey

Before anything else, preparation is the key to success
— Alexander Graham Bell

Before embarking on a difficult journey you need to make the necessary preparations. You have to purchase the right tools and learn how to use them. You need to bring along enough energy to get you to your destination. Searching for a man is no different. You need to prepare yourself physically and mentally. If you don't, you won't succeed.

The right frame of mind is key. Imagine you're looking for a job. You've probably done it at least once in your life, and know what it entails. You need to be proactive in your search. Just posting your resume on an online job board won't cut it. You need to network with everyone and anyone in the hope that someone will think of you when they hear of a job opening. You need to go to job fairs and networking events and work the crowd with a lot of determination, and a smile. You need to go on lots of interviews dressed for success and prepared to impress. You need to follow up with people in a timely manner. You can't get lazy, because there are lots of others who are competing for the same job you want. Most importantly, you need to stay positive. Negative thoughts can smash your confidence and ruin your chances of success.

Everything I just described about searching for a job applies to searching for a man. You need to get out, meet new people and network. Tell them you're looking and ask if they know someone appropriate. Follow up with them to make sure they keep you in mind. Go to events and work the crowd. Go on dates and impress.

I'll go over all of the items I just mentioned in greater detail later in the book, but for now all you need to remember is that you need to take your love search as seriously as you would a job search. Most singles don't. They suddenly become religious and leave their fate up to God. "Whatever is meant to be will be" and "If God wants me to meet Mr. Right, it'll happen regardless of where I am or what I do." Wrong. God does want you to meet Mr. Right, but it's your job to make it happen.

Determination

I worked with a woman who desperately wanted to get married. She was very attractive and had no shortage of eager suitors. The problem was that she was looking for a specific type of man that was not readily available in her particular social circle. She was super determined to succeed. She made finding her man her number one priority. She contacted everyone she knew to let them know she was looking, and she followed up with them regularly. She networked her pretty behind off wherever she went. She was relentless. It was frustrating. She had some false alarms and disappointments. She could have easily slipped into a more passive role or just plain given up. She didn't. She believed in her vision and was determined to succeed against all odds. Her hard work finally paid off. One of the amateur matchmakers she regularly hounded happened to hear about a guy in a city over 1000 miles away who had just become available and who she thought would be a good fit. Yes, they got married. I believe that it was this woman's hard work and raw determination that made it happen. She never stopped pushing. That's the state of mind you need to put yourself in to find your Mr. Right.

You don't want to come across as desperate, right? Not to worry. There's a difference between determination and desperation. Determination is positive. You want something important and are willing to do whatever it takes to get it. Desperation is almost the same except for the way you go about getting what you want. A determined person always retains her dignity and self respect in her drive towards her objective. She asks for help. She never begs. She takes chances and becomes vulnerable, but never at the expense of her self-worth and integrity. She gains the respect of those she comes into contact with, who admire her for her efforts. She never feels embarrassed or ashamed. A desperate woman lacks that dignity and self respect. She makes people feel uncomfortable. She evokes pity. A determined woman is attractive. A desperate woman is anything but. Be determined, not desperate.

Attitude

Attitude is another important item in your search toolkit. A positive attitude will help you succeed. A negative one will break you. Most people want to be around positive people. If you had the choice of spending an evening with a dark, gloomy sort of man who complained about everything and everyone, or an upbeat, energetic guy with a positive outlook on life, who would you choose?

I'm not telling you to put on an act and prance around like a Hare Krishna love child on crack. Just be positive. Don't sit across the table from your date bitching about how you hate the whole singles scene and how all fashion models should be force fed and executed. Just smile and try to find the bright side of life, or at least the topic under discussion. You can't imagine how attractive a positive attitude will make you seem in the eyes of potential mates as well as potential referrals.

I know a woman who I think is attractive and personable. Whenever I run into her she's got a mouthful to say about how hard it is to meet anyone or how hopeless the singles scene is. Her whole demeanor is negative. It's like a dark cloud is hovering over her, all the time. Come to think of it, I think I dated her once or twice years ago, and felt like slitting my wrist and leaping out of my seventh floor window after the date. If she had changed her attitude, things might have worked out differently. You never know. Be positive.

Relax

I know a woman who is just a bundle of nerves. I'm sure you do to. It's not very attractive. She's always got this troubled, uptight look about her, as if she's waiting for her doctor to tell her the results of a recent biopsy. There might be some men who go for that needy, distressed thing. Most don't. She needs to relax. So do you.

Just about everyone gets nervous in stressful situations. It's understandable. For many men and women, dating is one of those situations. I speak from personal experience. For the first decade of my dating journey I was too nervous to eat on a first, second, and sometimes even a third date. Of course that was only when I liked the girl. If I wasn't interested I could devour both of our meals and dessert. I did my best to meet my dates for drinks or to arrange some sort of fun or interesting activity, where I could relax and be my charming self. But sometimes I had no alternative to the dreaded dinner thing. I think I was pretty good at covering up my anxiety, but I suspect that plenty of my dates picked up on my discomfort and decided to forgo a second act.

I'm no psychologist, and I assume that everyone has their own causes for their anxiety so I won't try to offer any cures. All I can do is tell you how I got over my early date anxiety disorder. I recognized that I only had my problem with women I was interested in. I desperately wanted to win their favor. I was afraid of *blowing it*. In my mind I turned every date into an audition or job interview. I gave the poor girl sitting across from me the power to judge me as worthy or unworthy of her continued attention. Every date became a new theatre stage or HR office. My performance anxiety would subside only when I felt that I had gotten the job or the part, which usually took anywhere from three to five dates.

At some point in my mid thirties, I started to feel confident about myself. I realized that I couldn't control how others viewed me. That was their business. All I could do was be the best ME that I could be. If the woman I was with didn't like what she saw, then she obviously wasn't right for me. The right woman would like me for who I was, as is. I stopped letting myself be judged and started enjoying being myself. My anxiety disappeared. Dating became fun instead of stressful. I started getting a lot more second and third dates. I also gained a few pounds in the process, and thoroughly enjoyed each one.

While solving the root of your anxiety is the best way to go, it could be a long process. So you need some short term solutions to get you through your soulmate search while you work on the big stuff. Even if you're not struggling with anxiety, the suggestions and techniques I'll describe are great for just staying fit, both physically and mentally.

Exercise

It's scientifically proven that exercise relieves stress. How exactly it does that isn't altogether clear. One thing we know is that more than twenty minutes of continuous exercise causes your body to produce endorphins, which uplift your mood and make you feel mighty fine. Walking, running, swimming, and biking are great ways to get your endorphins flowing. Pick an aerobic activity you enjoy, do it every day, and watch your stress and anxiety melt away.

Breathe

If you weren't breathing you'd be dead. But unless it's a near death experience you're looking for, those occasional, shallow breaths are not going to make you feel more relaxed. According to scientific studies, deep, full breaths will. All you need to do is inhale, hold, and exhale. There are lots of different breathing exercises you can learn but they're all based on the basic inhale, hold, exhale, and repeat. Try it now:

Step 1: Breathe in deeply through your nose allowing your stomach to expand, for four counts

Step 2: Hold the breath for four counts

Step 3: Exhale through your mouth allowing your stomach to drop, for four counts

Step 4: Hold for four counts

Step 5: Repeat

As you release your breath imagine that you're expelling all the anxious and stressful energy in your body. You can repeat this simple breathing exercise until you feel more relaxed. If this particular exercise doesn't work for you, there are hundreds of others out there for you to choose from.

Visualize

The human mind has trouble differentiating between the real and the imagined. The mechanism your mind and body put into motion when faced with a vividly imagined danger is the same as if the danger was real. Just think of your last horror movie or nightmare. Luckily, the same principle applies to pleasure. Vivid images can make you feel the same degree of pleasure as real life physical contact. If you think positive thoughts, you will transform yourself into a positive person. If you think relaxed, you'll become relaxed. If you feel nervous about how you'll act on a date, play it out in your imagination before you go. Visualize yourself saying all the right things and being relaxed, positive, and energetic. Now that you've virtually experienced a successful date, you'll feel confident and relaxed when you go live.

Sleep

The amount of sleep you get directly effects your mood and energy level. Getting too much sleep is usually not the problem. Most people get too little. Skimping on your snoozing time can make you nervous, depressed, cranky, grouchy, and just plain unpleasant to be around. You can do without the late show. Set your DVR and get some sleep. Your social life will thank you.

Kick Back

Take some time out to just chill. Do something you enjoy. Read a good book, watch TV, stroll in the park, have coffee with friends. Get your mind off the stresses in your life and just enjoy living. You'll feel happier and radiate positive energy to those around you.

Affirm

Make a list of the things about yourself that you're proud of. Things that you're good at. Things that you like about yourself. Read them out loud and affirm your self-worth. Feel good about yourself.

As the Buddha said, "You, yourself, as much as anybody in the entire universe, deserve your love and affection."

Chapter Four

Appearance Counts

Everything has beauty, but not everyone sees it.

— Confucius

My wife always reminds me, "every pot has its cover." That means everyone will find their match regardless of how they look. There might be some truth to that. But I'm a rationalist, an enlightened man of science, bound by the rules of probability and statistics. That, along with my experience speaking with hundreds of men, compels me to say that the overwhelming majority of American men are primarily focused on how a potential mate looks.

Ok, I can hear the curses and feel the death stares (sorry honey) but I will not buckle to the pressure at the expense of your future happiness. My sole objective is to help you find your Mr. Right, so I plow onward.

According to a study conducted by psychologists from a North Carolina University published in the Journal of Personality and Social Psychology, men are particularly attracted to women who look thin and seductive. You didn't need a scientific study to give you that piece of information. Just look at the most distinguished publication aimed at sophisticated male readers: Playboy. The average Playboy Playmate is 5 feet 6 inches tall and weighs 115 pounds, with a BMI of 8.5. Do all men want to date women who look like Playboy Playmates? Do you really want me to answer that (knowing that my wife is reading this)?

Let's just say that many American men are attracted to women who are relatively thin. I precede "thin" with "relatively" because there is a range of acceptability among men regarding the definition of thin. Some men consider thin to be of the runway model variety, while others allow it to include just a few extra pounds, in the right places of course. There are plenty of men who like a well padded *tush* and hips and plenty who don't. Hell, there are men who like obese women. But if you want to play the odds and have the most options you need to bet on the thinner side.

Getting into better shape shouldn't be something you do just to attract a man. Eating healthier and smarter and exercising should be part of everyone's lifestyle. You'll feel better and live longer. But sticking to our topic, I guarantee you that your dating life will improve. It might be because you drop a few pounds and attract different men or maybe because you feel more energetic and give off a more positive vibe. It doesn't really matter why, as long as it works.

True Story 1

I knew a woman named Karen who was friends with someone I was dating. Karen was an attorney in her late twenties, smart, witty and a real sweetheart. She was also tall, attractive and relatively thin. But looking at her through the super critical eyes of many of the men in her social circle, she had a few extra pounds on her core. Like I said, she could by no means be considered heavy or overweight, but when stacked up against her "competitors", she looked a lot bigger than she was. I can't say for sure, but I think it was hurting her dating life, which in turn made her seem kind of sad, at least every time I saw her. That down energy probably didn't help her cause much either.

Karen started running. Maybe it was to lose weight, maybe just to relieve stress and feel better. A few months later I bumped into her on her way home from one of her runs. Wow, what a change. She was thin, by anyone's definition. I gotta tell you, she looked amazing. In fact, I think I did tell her that. She was also happy (and sweaty!). Not too long after that I heard that Karen got engaged. Was it because she lost weight? Was it because she felt more energetic and positive? Was it purely a coincidence? We'll never know for sure, but I think the running had something to do with it.

True Story 2

I once worked with a woman named Donna, who was in her mid 20's, tall, and overweight. She had a lovely face and an energetic personality. We met a couple of time to discuss how she could improve her dating life and meet the right guy. I felt that her weight was a major obstacle in her search and I decided that I had to tell her, for her own good. I'll admit I dreaded having that conversation with her and was scared she'd be insulted and hurt. I mustered up the courage, looked her in the eye, and told her that I thought that if she worked on losing some weight she would increase her odds at meeting someone. She responded that she had a rare hormonal condition, inherited from her mother, which made her gain weight. "I was thin as a model in college," she said. But then the condition kicked in and the weight began to pile on and there was little she could do. She did say, however, that it might be possible for her to lose a few pounds, but it would take a tremendous amount of effort and discipline, way beyond the norm.

Well, that's what I get for opening my big mouth. I felt terrible, but Donna thanked me for being honest and promised to think about what I had said. Not long after our meeting Donna called me to say that I had motivated her to start a new diet. A few months later, she had lost around 20 pounds, was looking thinner, and feeling great. Soon after, I heard she got engaged. Was it because of the weight loss? I don't think it was a coincidence.

Whether you agree with me or not, you've really got nothing to lose (except for a few pounds), and possibly a lot to gain from improving your diet and overall state of fitness. At the very least you'll be fitter and feel healthier. What's wrong with that?

When it comes to hairstyles, hair color, and clothing styles, I'm pretty clueless. So are most men. Different men like different things. Some like blondes with straight hair and other brunettes with curls. There's no right answer to, "what kind of hair or clothing do men prefer?" Men want women who look pretty, however they define that term. Your mission, if you choose to accept it, is to try to look the best that you can based on what God gave you to work with.

If you can figure out how to do that on your own, great. If not, then you should ask someone who can advise you.

You can ask a girlfriend to advise you, but only if you're positive that she will be totally honest with you. If your friend or roommate always tells you that you look great in everything you wear, you need to be suspicious. She might be afraid to hurt you, or she might only see your inner beauty (which your date might miss), or she might even be a little jealous and want you to look like a sack of potatoes. A male friend is probably your best source of critique, but only if you're sure he's comfortable being totally honest with you. Many guys won't risk hurting you by telling you exactly how they see things. Maybe your brother?

My advice is to pay for some expert advice. A professional image consultant will be objective. That's his or her job. They'll tell you which hairstyle will work for your particular facial structure and which will make you look like a Sesame Street puppet. They'll tell you what to wear to accentuate your good points and hide your challenging ones. One or two meetings should be enough to get you on the right track and enable you to move forward on your own. There are also lots of helpful videos on the internet that you can learn and get ideas from.

However you decide to do it, make sure you learn how to look your best all the time. And don't forget to smile. You'll feel more confident and positive about yourself, and you'll make finding your Mr. Right a lot smoother and more enjoyable.

Chapter Five

When It's Time to Change

The truth is that our finest moments are most likely to occur when we are feeling deeply uncomfortable, unhappy or unfulfilled. For it is only in such moments, propelled by our discomfort, that we are likely to step out of our ruts and start searching for different ways or truer answers.

— M. Scott Peck

Have you ever observed a fly trying to get out of a room through an open window? The fly will often continue banging into the glass, when all it has to do is move just an inch to the side to set itself free. A mentor of mine pointed this out to me to make me realize that I was continuing to do the same things over and over with no success, instead of making a change, even a slight adjustment, and changing the course of my life. I was blown away by the lesson, but it took me a long time and a lot of internal struggle before I could implement the advice.

If you've been dating for more than a few years and still haven't found that committed relationship you desire, you need to take some time to reevaluate. It's possible that you're doing everything right and that factors beyond your control have messed things up for you. But maybe it's you. If you've been doing your thing in your particular way for years without achieving your goal, then you need to seriously consider making a change. This applies to all aspects of life, including career and life goals, and especially dating.

Reading this book is a start. It'll give you some good advice and guidance. But you probably have to go further, deeper. You need to conduct a brutally honest self-evaluation to figure out what you need to do differently to improve your situation. You might get your inspiration and insight from this book, or a mentor, or you might just come to it on your own. However you get there the important thing is to make a change. How much of a change, how drastic, how large or small is totally up to you. It's your life. Just don't be that fly that keeps banging into that same glass pane. Make an adjustment. Make a change.

The most drastic change I made was when I decided to take a few months and travel to Israel with a clear mission: to find my life partner. I had thought, talked, and even dreamed about it, but for a decade and a half I lived my life the same comfortable way I always had. Yes, I did make adjustments along the way, and I saw tangible results, but I needed to make that big change to really succeed. Why I decided to make that particular decision isn't important. What matters is that I tore myself out of my comfort zone and made a change I felt I needed to make. I met my wife a few days after I landed.

Change isn't easy. Most of us strive to attain a comfort level in life. When we achieve it, we dread losing it. The older we get, the more comfortable we get in our familiar routine, and the harder it gets to make a change. It's scary, but you can do it. I promise you, you can change your life. The most important thing is to make that decision to change, and commit to seeing it through, no matter how hard it may seem at first. It will always be easier to continue, or fall back, on the path you're currently on and comfortable with. If you choose to do that you'll continue to be comfortable, but frustrated and unhappy. You have the power to change your life. Use it.

Homework

Take some quality time to evaluate yourself. Your life. What has gone right and what hasn't. Why did things turn out the way they did? Review specific situations. Understand them. Then figure out what you could have done to make the not so good events turn out differently. Is there something particular you can change about yourself, how you act, how you treat people?

SECTION TWO

FINDING HIM

Chapter Six

Strategy for Success

No idea is so outlandish that it should not be considered with a searching but at the same time a steady eye.

— Winston Churchill

One of the questions I'm asked most often is: Where can I find the kind of man I'm looking for? They want me to reveal to them those secret, "off market", locations hidden from the average single, where the beautiful and successful come to mingle and match. If they could just gain entry to that Fantasy Island utopia of fireworks studded, chemistry filled, love at first sight matches, they would finally find the "right one". Do I have an address, even a clue, something, anything? Please?

As far as I know, there is no cupid Garden of Eden where meeting your soulmate is guaranteed. There are single men just about everywhere. But you're not just looking for any single man. You're looking for a man who will satisfy most of the items on your I

Do List. You've put a lot of soul searching and effort into refining your list to make it reflect who you really are. You've removed the items that are irrelevant for a happy marriage. You're even willing to compromise on a few of the remaining items that are not critical to marital success. You've made your decision to date for marriage. You've prepared yourself mentally and physically. You're focused, energetic, positive, and determined to succeed in your search. Now where the hell is he?

One popular strategy for finding your man is the indiscriminate or "you never know" strategy. You never know where he might be, so you need to look everywhere. You need to attend every event no matter how inappropriate you think it might be because, you never know. You need to go out with every guy thrown your way even if the person setting you up is your blind, 88 year old next door neighbor who swears on the lives of her five cats that her nephew is the handsomest young actuary to ever open his own funeral home. You just never know.

I don't recommend that you follow the "you never know" strategy. You could win the lottery, but I wouldn't recommend you quit your job hoping that'll happen because the odds of you winning are much too miniscule to depend on. Searching for the right man is no different. You might counter with, "I've got nothing to lose if I go out with him." I disagree. You've got plenty to lose.

Every bad date you go on has its price. The most obvious is time. You can cut that time down to a bare minimum, but it's still a block of time I know you could use more productively than spending with a stranger you've determined, based on your list, is not a potential partner. Your time is valuable. Don't waste it.

A bad date can also sap your energy, leaving you frustrated and depressed. You've built up all this positive energy only to come home from your bad date saying, "there's no one out there for me", "maybe I should just settle for this guy even if he is totally wrong for me", "how many more of these am I going to have to go on to meet the right guy?"

The worst thing that could happen is that you go out with a guy you know does not match your I Do List, and then fall for him. You'll either end up wasting a lot of time, possibly years, and suffer through a tremendous amount of emotional pain, or end up in an unhappy marriage or unpleasant divorce. I've seen this happen so many times. It rarely ends well. Trust your I Do List.

The strategy I'm suggesting you use to find your Mr. Right is what I call Sticking to Your I Do List As If Your Life Depended On It. It's simple. Don't waste your time on men that don't meet your primary I Do List items. It doesn't matter how handsome, successful, or downright saintly they are. Date only those men who fit your bill. No Exceptions.

Let's say you're Jewish and you've indicated on your I Do List that you will only marry someone Jewish. (Hey, I'm a rabbi, what did you think I'd say?) When your sweet old Catholic landlady Mary McDonald offers to fix you up with her handsome son Chris, the CEO of a large investment firm, you politely decline. It doesn't matter how much money he makes or how good looking he is. Trust your list. And don't just date for fun. That isn't fair to either of you.

The challenge of sticking to your I Do List is that you will date a whole lot less and be alone a whole lot more. That's not a bad thing, it's just challenging for many women who might equate not having dates to not being desirable. You're not a loser if you're alone because you're trusting your I Do List. You're a winner because you're saving yourself a lot of wasted time, energy, and frustration. But I'll admit, it can be a hard strategy to stick to. In my own dating experience there were times when I didn't date for months at a time. It wasn't because I couldn't get a date or because there were no attractive women to ask. I could, and there were. I just knew that none of those women fit my I Do List, and at that point in my life, I fully trusted my list. As much as I wanted the company and the fun, I stayed strong and held fast to my strategy. I really believe it paid off in the end, and will for you too.

What do you do while you're staying true to your I Do List and not going out on dates?

Friends and Family

Work on building and strengthening the relationships in your life that matter to you that tend to be pushed to the side when you're dating.

Take Care of You

Do the things you enjoy doing. The things that make you happy. Read a good book. Get a massage. Exercise. Take a trip. Have fun!

Network

Continue your love search by going to events, parties, and all sorts of interesting activities that you enjoy, where you can meet people and expand your network. You might even get lucky.

Do not slip into indiscriminate dating. Stay strong and trust your I Do List.

Dating Alert

If you feel like you're going for much too long without a date, you should reevaluate your I Do List just to make sure you aren't being unrealistic.

Chapter Seven

Looking for Love in All the Right Places

Flaming enthusiasm, backed up by horse sense and persistence, is the quality that most frequently makes for success. -

— Dale Carnegie

Now that you're focused on dating only the right men and steering clear of the ones who don't match your I Do List, the next step is to find the men you're seeking. To do that you need to do your market research. Are we talking business or love? I'm not selling a product, I'm looking for a man! Well, I hate to break this to you, but you are selling a product: YOU. You need to find the customers who are interested in the product you're selling. How do you find customers, short of taking out personal ads? By thoroughly researching the singles "market" to figure out where to find your target man. Let's work through an example.

You've decided that your Mr. Right is college educated, works in an artistic field, loves city life, and is active in social causes.

50

If you live in a big city, you're on the right track. If you live on a farm in rural Kansas, you should seriously consider moving. The odds are against you finding your man at the local barn dance. So you Google singles events in your city of choice and your top results are:

> ➢ Wall Street Young Professionals Cocktails
> ➢ Art Exhibit Meet and Greet
> ➢ Save the Whale Fundraising Picnic

The first one's easy, right? You're looking for someone who works in the arts, so the Wall Street thing is off target. Yeah, the guys there make a lot of money and you always do real well with this crowd...STOP. You are not going. You are focusing, remember? Try to match the guy you're seeking with the type of event or activity he might choose to attend. If you're looking for a guy who loves the outdoors, focus on activities like hikes or rafting trips.

Choices two and three look like winners. They might be, but you need to do some more research to make sure you don't waste time, money, and precious positive energy. Try to find out what kind of guys go to these events, or if guys go to them at all. You don't want to walk into the Art Exhibit to find it filled with pretty ladies and gay gentlemen. That wouldn't do much for your dating life. You also don't want to go to the picnic and find it filled with aging flower children, unless you're looking for an "older" man.

Your research should focus on the type of crowd that usually attends the event you're evaluating. You want to get as specific as possible. Generally how old are the men that come? Is it a "cool" crowd, or "not so cool" with a capital L? You get this information through word of mouth. This is one of the main reasons why networking to make new male and female friends is important. The wider your social circle the more information you can gather and the less time you'll waste.

Most events have Facebook pages where you can usually see who is invited and who is coming. In fact, Facebook is probably the best tool for determining whether the crowd attending will be a good fit for you. If you don't have any friends that can guide you and the event isn't on Facebook, it's probably not a good sign. Seriously, who isn't on Facebook? As a last resort you can just speak directly to the event organizer and try to get an honest answer.

When I get those calls asking me for the right singles events or venues, I respond that I honestly have no idea. I'm married. I don't go to singles events anymore so how am I supposed to know where the right ones are for you? You need to get to work and do your due diligence. All the information you'll need is out there on the web and among your friends. But you need to put the effort into finding the right stuff and analyzing it.

What about just getting out there and meeting people wherever you are, like at Starbucks, the local supermarket, or even on the street? You could certainly try, but even if you do get lucky and meet someone, you'll have no idea whether they fit any part of your I Do List other than the physical attraction item. That could end up costing you lots of wasted time and heartache down the road.

The only way I'm going to let you just go out there and meet someone is if you target venues where you've determined your man might be. That at least gives you a fighting chance at meeting someone appropriate. You can then target even more based on what he's reading, the clothing he's wearing, and the people he's with. As long as you're targeting, you can roam the city on your love search. You never know.

Chapter Eight

Network, Network, Network

A friend may well be reckoned the masterpiece of nature.

— Ralph Waldo Emerson

The dictionary definition of the verb network is to cultivate people who can be helpful professionally, especially in finding employment or moving to a higher position. Let's modify that definition to apply to dating: to cultivate people who can introduce you to, or help you meet, your Mr. Right.

You already know what networking is. You probably do it all the time. I just want to emphasize how important it is to your love search. The more people you connect with, the greater the chance that one of them might know someone appropriate for you to date. Networking with other singles at events or in social settings is easy, because you don't have to explain your objective to them. They're in the same boat. They get it. Networking with non singles or even with singles in professional settings is more difficult, because you need to clearly articulate your request for assistance.

I know lots of women who are anxious to tell anyone and everyone that they're single and eager to date. I'm thinking of one in particular. Jennie is super attractive and personable, and has no trouble getting dates, but for one reason or another (usually not of her doing), things haven't worked out for her yet. Whenever she speaks with people who she thinks might be able to introduce her to new men, she asks. She does so in an upbeat, positive, and confident way that makes them feel excited to help. There's not a trace of desperation or pity seeking. She realizes that searching for her soulmate is nothing to be ashamed of or embarrassed about.

Some women feel differently. They think that asking for help is admitting that they don't have what it takes to find a man on their own. If they did, wouldn't they have found one already and be on the other end of the conversation? They imagine their married friends looking at them with pity saying, "isn't it so sad that she's still in that horrible dating scene instead of being home with a husband and children?" While that might be true in some cases, in most it just isn't. Most people sincerely want to help you if they can, period. Instead of pity, they're probably a bit envious of your freedom and independence, especially when they're waking up in the middle of the night to change diapers or dealing with screaming kids and household chores while severely sleep deprived. I'm not saying I would trade my wife and kids for anything, but I have to admit, I do sometimes miss the freedom of my single days.

If you feel uncomfortable asking for help, despite what you just read, I understand. I felt the same way when I was single. I dreaded asking for help for fear of seeming inadequate. I was good enough to find my soulmate on my own. I eventually did, but my stubbornness and fear cost me many more years of being alone. Are you willing to postpone the next stage of your life to protect your ego from a threat that doesn't even exist, or at worst, doesn't matter?

Cheryl, a woman I worked with, refuses to reach out to her friends and acquaintances to ask them to help her find her man. She rarely meets guys on her own, and the ones she does meet are not good matches for her. I told her that I think the right man for her is outside of her immediate social circle and neighborhood and that she needs to network with people in other locations (which I identified) where I think her man might be found. She needs to reconnect with old friends and acquaintances whom she hasn't been in touch with for years who live in those target locations and ask them for assistance. She's too embarrassed or proud to do that. So she's still spinning her wheels in her same old situation, hoping for a miracle. She's choosing pride over happiness.

Social media has made networking easier and more productive than ever. You can expand your network and reach people you would have never been able to before. On Facebook you not only have your own network, but you can also see all of your friends' networks and try to expand your own based on your connection to them. The best thing is that you can do it all without having to make an actual phone call or have an embarrassing conversation. You do have to pick up the phone eventually but at least you can first test the waters to weed out those unable or unwilling to help. I actually met my wife through the FB network, but I'll tell you about that a bit later on.

Networking for dating assistance in a professional setting is a point of contention. Some say absolutely not. There's a time and place for everything, and a business event is not the place for dating networking. Others say it's fair game, as long as you keep the conversation appropriate. In my opinion the right answer is somewhere in the middle. In general I agree that if you're a participant at a business or professional event you should stick to business and leave your social requests for the late night after-party. But there are always exceptions. If your business conversation takes a personal turn and you feel comfortable, then go for it. You've gotta feel the moment. Of course, if the guy you're shmoozing with happens to be single and cute, fits your list, and doesn't work with you, to heck with the rules. What have you got to lose? If he's a co-worker, read chapter 13 to find out how to proceed.

If you were looking for a job to survive, you would network your butt off and ask everyone for help. If you're determined to find a potential marriage partner, you need to do the same. Don't be desperate. Be confident. Be positive. Your contacts will admire your determination, and hopefully give you some good leads.

Chapter Nine

Matchmakers

I love her too, but our neuroses just don't match.

— Arthur Miller

The ancient art of matchmaking has experienced a resurgence in recent years. No longer the exclusive domain of Type A personality Jewish grandmothers with Yiddish accents, today's matchmakers are mostly young, educated and attractive (Type A) professionals in touch with the modern dating environment. Most of them accept only male clients. Women are relegated to large harems of potential matches for their well to do *boychicks*. Most of these princes are looking for sexy, gorgeous, bubbly young ladies in their twenties to early thirties. If you feel you're up for that, give it a shot but realize that the competition is fierce and plentiful. You might even get the chance to be rejected on national television because your breasts are too small or your teeth aren't white enough. Just what you always dreamed of.

Don't give up yet. The matchmakers with the male clients are the ones trying to make a living at it, and there aren't too many of them. (Are you surprised that only a small number of men are willing to pay to be set up?) There are lots of matchmakers out there, mostly female, who do it just for the satisfaction they get from making people happy, even if it is only a small handful who actually meet and marry. Some of them know what they're doing. Some of them are clueless.

I know one of the good ones. She's a marketing professional turned stay at home mom in New York City, and she absolutely loves setting people up. She doesn't charge a penny, she's a real pleasure to speak with, and she makes you feel good. I recommend her to some of my clients because I know she understands the reality of the dating scene. She won't waste your time with dates that she knows won't work. That's important. If you can find one of the good ones, you've got nothing to lose by asking them to work their magic for you.

You don't have to be a professional matchmaker to make matches. Almost everyone enjoys introducing two people who they think might hit it off. Many of them won't do it unless asked, for fear of insulting you by implying that you can't meet someone on your own. That's why you always have to make it clear that you're ready, willing, and able to be matched and will consider any suggestions. This doesn't mean you have to go out with everyone suggested to you. You need to make sure they fit your trusted I Do List. If they don't, tell your matchmakers how much you really appreciate their efforts and politely decline. Explain why you're declining, so that they'll know better for the future. Be as honest as you can. The more information they have the better suggestions they can make.

It's important to share your I Do List with any potential matchmaker. A good one will insist that you do. Matchmakers will often try to fit you into preexisting categories they can easily understand and work with. They'll compare their first impression of you with the stereotypes they're familiar with, until you give them reason to do otherwise. They'll ask you general questions about who you are and what you're looking for, but it's your job to reveal to them the *real* you that they won't get from a superficial interview. You can hide almost anything from an interviewer if you're careful, and many people do. But what are you left with then? Lots of off base suggestions and bad dates. The more you share the better the matches you'll get.

After you do go out on a date set up by a matchmaker or friend, you should provide them with detailed feedback. The more detailed the better. Just saying he wasn't right or wasn't a good fit is not enough. You need to explain why. When you do, be prepared to hear a rebuttal. A good matchmaker won't just make the match. He or she will try to coach you through the dating process. I think this is where the real value of a good matchmaker shines through. You can't beat having an experienced pro by your side to make you think twice before discarding a potential mate.

What if your good friend sets you up with her brother-in-law and he turns out to be a real creep? Ok, you can be ambiguous and just say you didn't feel the chemistry. Don't tell her the truth.

Will you damage your relationship with your matchmaking friends if you pass on their suggestions because they're off base? In most cases probably not. They might stop setting you up, which won't be such a bad thing based on their track record. You need to be true to yourself. If you feel that their suggestion for you is wrong, then respect your decision. They should too.

One last point about matchmakers or matchmaking friends. You need to follow up with them to remind them you're still alive and searching. Matchmakers deal with lots of singles. The top ones might have hundreds or thousands in their database. Your friends have busy lives. If you want to be remembered by your dating agents you need to nudge them a little. I said a little, no daily messages or stalking. I speak from experience. I've got a bunch of people on my setup list, but the one I remember is the last one I just spoke to. One guy I worked with, who subsequently got married, would call me every Friday to wish me a good Sabbath. I heard he did that to a lot of people. He wasn't usually at the top of my list, but his weekly phone call pushed him back up there, at least for the weekend.

You never know who might be able to introduce you to your potential mate. Treat those who try with respect. Give them the information they need to make an accurate match. Follow up with them regularly. And don't forget to thank them for their efforts.

Chapter Ten

Finding Mr. Right Online

Will it be well with you when he searches you out?

— Job 26:1

Ideally, you'd love to meet the man of your dreams while sipping a latte at your local Starbucks or while standing in line at the supermarket. You'd even settle for a crowded party or bar. But the chances of that happening to you in the immediate future are too uncertain to bet on. You need to increase your odds of success. Enter: online dating.

Online dating gives you the opportunity to meet potential dating partners you would otherwise never get the chance to meet. You can also see their photos and get to know them a bit via email or chat. No longer are you confined to dating the men in your zip code. The world is your singles bar! Sure, there are pitfalls and dangers in the world of cyberdating, which we'll discuss in Chapter 18, but the opportunities are too inviting to ignore. You don't want to miss out on meeting that visiting Danish prince seeking an American bride, do you?

So how do you meet your potential mate online? You've got two options: social media sites and dating sites. You can choose both.

The largest and most popular social media site is Facebook. In my opinion it's also the best online dating site, and it's free. I'm not referring to the individual dating applications that you can download on the site. Those are only as good as the people that download and use them. I'm talking about Facebook in general, half a billion members and growing. But you're thinking, Facebook isn't a dating site. My parents and little sister are on it! You're right, it's not a traditional dating site. It's a powerful social networking tool that you can use to search for and meet potential mates, and it's a heck of a lot bigger and more effective than any dating site out there.

Figuring out how to use Facebook to meet potential dates isn't rocket science. If you haven't done so already, go through your list of friends to make sure you haven't missed any potential soulmates staring you right in the cyber-face. You'd be surprised how many Facebook friends you have that you don't really know or have never actually met. I accept friend requests from just about anyone who seems normal and wants to be my friend, for whatever reason, whether I know them or not. I'm sure you do the same. So go through your list and see if you can uncover some hidden gems.

Now go through your friends' lists. It's ok, that's the whole idea of social networking. If they didn't want you to see their friends they would have chosen the setting that prevents you from doing so. Check out each guy. If a particular profile photo catches your interest, click on it to view the underlying profile. Then click on "about" to see where they live and what their relationship status is. You won't always get the information you're seeking, either because it hasn't been entered or because non friends are blocked from viewing it. Not to worry. This is where the social networking piece of the puzzle comes into play. Once you've made a list of the people you think you'd like to meet, contact your friend and ask him or her about them.

Let's say you've identified Jim as someone you think is cute, but he doesn't have his relationship status on his profile. You contact your friend and ask about him.

"Hey, I happened to see that you're friends with Jim. Is he single? How well do you know him? Can you tell me a bit about him? Can you make an intro?"

If you like what you hear and your friend agrees to make an intro, hurray! You've now turned an online experience into an actual setup. If your friend doesn't feel comfortable making the intro, for whatever reason, check to see if you have any other mutual friends. If that doesn't work you can send Jim a friend request with a message introducing yourself as a friend of your mutual friend. Suddenly, your cold call email is not so cold anymore, because using your mutual friend connection has given you instant credibility. You're no longer some psycho stalker. You're a friend of a friend, and any friend of "mutual friend" must be ok.

Meeting a guy on Facebook is really even easier than I just described. If you've got an attractive profile photo, almost every single guy will accept your friend request, mutual friend or not. That's just how guys operate. A pretty picture will get their adrenalin rocking and their fantasies rolling. In most cases you won't have to do anything besides clicking that friend request button. They'll take it from there.

If he doesn't accept your friend request he's almost definitely not interested. There's a slight possibility that he isn't an active Facebook user and just hasn't seen your message. In that case you can try to find another mutual friend to introduce you offline or you can try finding out where he hangs out and just bump into him there. Whatever you do, please don't send him more Facebook messages or "poke" him.

If he does accept your request, it doesn't necessarily mean that he's interested in dating you. Like I said, lots of Facebook users accept anyone who doesn't seem threatening. But all is not lost. By becoming his Facebook friend you've gained the ability to see his wall, photos, and status updates (if you couldn't see them already). You can use this information to learn more about him and to try and find common interests to connect with. You can comment on his posts, invite him to events, and "like" his updates. As long as you don't go overboard, occasional strategically placed comments and "likes" can grab his attention in a very positive way. But you need to think about what you say and do, and make sure you don't completely destroy your chances with him by writing something stupid or inappropriate. If you're not sure what to write, skip it and just click on the "like" icon. It won't make as strong an impression as a witty or insightful comment, but it might catch his attention enough to get him to check out your profile.

If you think I'm totally off on my Facebook dating strategy, think again. It's how I met my wife. Before I embarked on my Israel wife seeking mission, I did my research. I had a handful of Facebook friends who lived in Israel, including one woman who I had dated some years before but was still friendly with. I went through her friend list and identified two women I found attractive. I looked at their profiles and noticed that they were both single. I then contacted my friend and asked about them. She didn't know either that well, but from what she did know, she thought that one was more up my alley than the other, but she didn't feel comfortable introducing us. So I sent the mystery woman a friend request with a message introducing myself as a friend of our mutual friend. She responded positively, and the rest is history. I guess I owe Mark Zuckerberg a shout out. Thanks Mark!

Dating Sites

Whether you love 'em or hate 'em, dating sites play a significant role in 21st century mating. On Facebook you can never be sure if the guy you're viewing is single and available. You're also limited to guys in your greater social network. Dating sites open you up to all of their members, whoever and wherever they might be, and you can assume that they're single. That's good and bad. The good part is that you can contact or be contacted by an authentic Danish prince seeking true love. The bad part is that there's probably no way a Danish prince is on your dating site. But every overweight, balding, unemployed loser who can't get a date is, and everyone of them is contacting you (sorry guys).

This is the main reason so many women are so frustrated with dating sites. They're sick of being inundated by messages from men they consider totally inappropriate, and being ignored by the guys they do want to meet. In the next chapter I'll show you how to create an online dating profile that will command attention, but that doesn't solve the problem of unwanted contacts.

I don't really have a solution. If you choose to be part of a dating site you need to be prepared to sift through the trash in the hope of finding some treasure. There are free dating sites with millions of members like Okcupid.com and POF.com (Plenty of Fish), huge paid membership sites like Match.com and Eharmony, and scores of niche sites based on religion, race, sexual orientation and almost any other differentiating factor you can think of. I won't comment on any of them because I just don't know them well enough. You can do your own due diligence before spending your hard earned cash. From my limited experience with online dating, I found that pretty much anyone on the paid sites was also on the free ones. Why they would do both isn't clear to me. I assume they were willing to gamble $10 to $30 a month on the off chance that their soulmate was only on the pay site. That's probably why many people continue to pay for the same thing they can get for free.

Am I telling you to close your paid dating site accounts? If you can spare the money and don't mind scrolling through the same old profiles and getting messages from inappropriate men, then by all means roll the dice and go for it. You might be one of the lucky ones to have your story featured on the homepage of one of those sites. As the wise man once said, even a broken clock is right twice a day.

But if you are one of the disappointed and frustrated who can't stop complaining about how much you hate online dating, then I have a word of advice for you: quit and spend your money on other things like quality singles events and trips, or a good dating coach or image consultant.

Chapter Eleven

Your Online Profile - Photos

Appearance rules the world.

— Friedrich Schiller

If you've chosen to play the online dating game, you need to make sure you've got a winning profile. Your profile is made up of photos and words. When the average man reviews the results of his online search, he only looks at the photos. If your photo catches his interest, he'll look at your age. If he's satisfied he'll view your entire profile. The first thing he'll focus on is your physical stats, like body type (thin, average, a few extra pounds), weight, and height. Only then will he read what you've written about yourself and what you're looking for.

It's shallow and short sighted, and you can't believe that an intelligent and sensitive guy would do that, but it's the truth. You can either ignore it and continue doing whatever it is you've been doing unsuccessfully, or you can accept it and do your best to play by the rules and win.

Most online dating profiles suck. I know, that's a bold statement and I've got no hard facts or statistics to back it up. Nevertheless, from my years of experience as a dater, matchmaker, and dating coach, I believe it to be accurate. Most profiles are just plain horrible. Those that aren't that bad, aren't that good either. That's good news for you, because if you follow my advice, you'll move way ahead of the rest of the online dating hordes.

If you're a professional model or look like one, you don't have much to worry about. Just snap the photo and be done with it. If you're not, don't get discouraged. You have full control over the photos you post. You don't need to worry about some photographer following you around, snapping candid shots when you least expect it. You can stage your photo shoot exactly the way you like. If you're not crazy about how you look from the neck down, you can just post a headshot. If you're ready to go full length (or anything in between), go for it. You're in control.

Do you need a professional photographer to take your profile photos? I'm probably going to ruffle some feathers and alienate some shutterbugs by saying this, but my answer is no. I do think that a good professional photographer who is creative and "hip" can definitely enhance how you appear in your photo (sans Photoshop!), but I think the creative and "hip" part is key here. I find many of those staged photos where you pose in front of a bright blue background leaning on a tree with a huge forced grin blatantly artificial and sometimes even a bit spooky. What you want is a photographer who can make you look your best *au naturale*. That takes talent.

I once attended a networking event where a professional photographer took headshots of the participants. I sat in front of a background, he told me to smile, turn left, turn right, done. I looked horrible in the photo! My smile was too big, my head wasn't tilted properly, it was just bad. Now I'm no model, but I've got lots of photos where I look pretty good and they were all taken by amateurs. Granted, lots of people looked really great in their headshots, but I wonder if they wouldn't have come out as good without a professional. Maybe not. It happened to have been a really good looking crowd so it's hard to tell what value the photographer added.

If you can find a photographer who you feel can really make you look natural and bring out your best, then by all means go for it. But if you can't or don't want to, no need to fret. As long as you have a friend with a decent camera who knows how to snap a photo, you're in business. You want your photo to be clear and well lit. You also want people to be able to recognize you, so don't standing half a mile away from the camera. On the other hand you don't want too close of a close up that highlights your old chicken pox scars and blackheads.

Setting

The setting of your photo can say a lot about you. A fun setting, like an amusement park, picnic, boat ride, or sporting event says, "I'm fun and active". The beauty of nature as your background says, "I'm real, down to earth, and love the great outdoors." A photo of you trekking in the Himalayas screams adventurous, while a shot of you working with children in India shows your caring side. Be creative with your setting to convey the aspect of your personality that you want potential partners to see.

Clothing

What you wear also speaks volumes about who you are and what you're looking for. Dressy, casual, sporty, hip, funky...it's all good, as long as it's sending the message you want to convey. If you're really gutsy you can use the photo of you in your Purim or Halloween costume (assuming it's attractive – no fruit or diapers). The first time I saw my wife's photo, on Facebook, she was wearing an Indian sari (her Purim costume), which succeeded in peaking my interest enough to contact her. No she didn't wear the sari on our first date, and yes, I was a bit disappointed (I've since gotten over it).

While the kind of clothing you wear doesn't really matter, as long as it reflects who you are, how you look in those clothes matters a heck of a lot. You want to make sure that you get the right type and fit of clothing for your particular look and body type. Not every woman can wear every type of clothing. Some styles, colors, and patterns are not flattering to some physical builds, sizes, and shapes. Find a friend or a professional who will be brutally honest and tell you what you should and shouldn't wear. A good image consultant who'll make you look good is worth more than a good photographer, so if you need to choose between the two, go image all the way. It'll be money well spent.

Hairstyle falls into the same category as clothing. Different folks look better or worse in different hairstyles. You need to figure out what works best for you. Don't be afraid to get a professional opinion. If you're not comfortable with your hair, or lack of it, you can always put on some sort of headgear or accessory. Nothing dishonest about a well placed baseball cap!

Smile

The only way you should appear in your photos is with a smile on your face. No one wants to be around a sourpuss. Even worse, some people look downright scary with a scowl on their face. The last thing you want to do is scare a potential partner off by looking like you should be on a wanted poster. No one in their right mind wants a relationship with the Upper West Side Stalker!

A smile radiates warmth, sincerity, self confidence, and happiness. It tells potential partners that they can expect an enjoyable, relaxed, and upbeat experience if they choose to date you. A non-smiling face screams NO FUN, STRESS, DRAMA, TENSION. Which face do you want to date? Obviously, there are different types and sizes of smiles, that each send a different message. A wide, toothy beam will radiate differently than a subtle, mysterious grin. You choose the kind that represents you best, but some form of positive facial expression is required.

I'll make a confession here and now: I'm a member of several online dating sites. Yes, my wife knows. No it's nothing weird or kinky. In order to continue to provide you with the best and most current dating advice, I need to know what's going on out there in the wild world of online dating. Sure I've got plenty of personal experience from my own dating journey (not that long ago), but it's really easy to forget, or block out, those "fun" times I spent scrolling through hundreds of profiles to find the one or two that actually grabbed my attention. So yes, I'm on some of the biggest and most popular sites (with no photo), so if you message someone and don't get a response, I apologize in advance if it was me.

I recently decided to take a look at the matches one of the free dating sites sent me. There were 45 profile photos on the page in front of me. A virtual smorgasbord of potential first dates to pick from. No one has the time or patience to click through to 45 individual profiles. When I saw the page of photos I was initially overwhelmed. I needed to filter through all those photos as quickly and efficiently as possible to find the ones I might be interested in.

Pay close attention to what I did next, because it is exactly what practically every other man will do in the same situation. You need to understand this in order to persuade a man to click on your photo instead of the other 44 vying for his attention.

As I scanned the photos one thing caught my eye and grabbed my attention: a smile. Any photo without a smiling woman was immediately disqualified. It wasn't premeditated. It was just a gut reaction I had. When I spent a moment thinking about it I realized that as a single man looking for a date, I don't want someone who's going to bring me down or make my life more complicated than it already is. I want someone who I can have fun with. Someone who'll make me happy. The ladies that were not smiling registered in my subconscious as downers. The smiling ladies said, "hey, I'm fun and can make you happy!".

That's not to say that after clicking on a photo and investigating a bit further I would have potentially dated each smiler. But one thing is clear: I did not pay any attention to the non-smiling photos. They didn't get the chance to impress me with their other profile photos or essays. I skipped right over them.

If you want to grab a man's attention and get him to click on your photo you've got two choices:

1. You can wear a bikini and show off your body (or other imaginative and seductive poses that highlight your assets). Even if you have what it takes to make that work for you, I can think of a few good reasons why, if you're looking for a serious relationship, you shouldn't.

2. Smile. I'd go with the smile every time. It tells a man you're happy and fun. That's what men want in a date. You'll have lots of opportunities to drive him crazy once you're in a relationship. Your goal now is to persuade the guy to pick your photo out of dozens or hundreds (thousands??) of others and click on it to learn more about you. My simple male mind advices you to smile.

One Singular Sensation

Your main profile photo should be of you alone, not you and your ex (or current) squeeze, or you and your best friends who happen to be better looking than you. You want it to be absolutely clear that it is YOU who is ready for a relationship, or at least a date. If the person viewing the photo can't figure out for sure who you are or decides to date your friend, you know you've messed up.

No Photo?

What if you feel, for whatever reason, that displaying your photo will be detrimental to your chances of attracting potential partners?

First of all, don't be so hasty in making that determination. Just because *you* think you look terrible doesn't mean others do. We've all heard of the super models and actresses who can't stand the way they look...yes, they exist. Maybe you're just being a bit too hard on yourself? It's not uncommon. Before you climb under that rock or call Dr. Plastic Makeover, get a second opinion from someone who you trust will be totally (brutally) honest.

If after performing your due diligence you still feel uncomfortable about putting your photo up for all to see, then don't. Understand that most potential partners will ignore your photo-less profile. However, if you are skilled in the written word and can create an incredibly engaging, interesting, and captivating written profile (which I'll explain how to do in the next section), you have a chance of attracting the attention of some of the more cerebral soulmate searchers out there. Let them rejoice in your exciting and intriguing personality, and deal with the photo when the time is right.

Dating Alert

Never post a photo of someone else (and say it's you) or a photo that is too old to truly represent how you actually look today.

The last piece of business you need to take care of regarding your profile photos has nothing to do with your online dating profile. It has to do with all the other photos you have floating around cyberspace. You see, most online daters won't stop at viewing your dating profile photos. They'll type your name into Google Images and look you up on Facebook. Then they'll examine each and every photo of you that's ever been posted anywhere in cyberspace. Any photo of you that doesn't portray you in the most attractive light will be held against you and be grounds for dismissal.

Get rid of all unflattering photos of you, wherever they live, especially Facebook. It doesn't matter if it's a shot of you at your best friend's wedding. If it doesn't meet your photo standards, take it down and save it for the day after your wedding. Your friend will understand. If someone else is posting photos that include you, make sure they meet your requirements and if they don't, ask your friends to take them down or just untag yourself.

Finally, if you notice that you're not getting much activity after several weeks, change your photos. Try a different pose, setting, outfit or facial expression (smile?!). Keep experimenting until you get it right.

Points to remember regarding online photos:

- ♥ Use a decent camera.
- ♥ Make sure the person taking your photo has a clue about how to use the camera and take a decent photo. Otherwise, use a professional.
- ♥ Use a current photo.
- ♥ Make sure you're the only one in your photo.
- ♥ Make sure people can see you and recognize you.
- ♥ Choose a setting that reflects your personality.
- ♥ Smile.
- ♥ Make sure you look good in every single one of your photos.

Now that you've got your profile photos in order, let's move on to your profile essays.

Chapter Twelve

Your Online Profile - Essays

There is nothing to writing. All you do is sit down at a typewriter and bleed.

— Ernest Hemingway

Your profile photos are what persuade men to consider contacting you. Your essays are what make a serious mate seeker hit send. It's in these paragraphs that you proclaim who you are, what you love and hate, and who you want to spend time (the rest of your life?) with. This is your opportunity to shine, dazzle, entice, and seduce. Remember, your goal is not to attract just anyone. You want to attract a potential partner that shares your life goals and dreams. The clearer and more open you are in expressing what those goals and dreams are and, most importantly, who YOU really are, the better chance you'll have of meeting the "right one".

Some dating sites let you write separate paragraphs for who you are and what you're looking for in a partner. Others make you put it all in one place. Either way is fine. All that matters is that you get your point across.

Style

Your writing style should ideally reflect your personality. It can be fun and witty, serious and introspective, playful and romantic, or however else you feel like expressing yourself.

The problem with writing in a creative is that unless you do it well, you can easily give off the wrong impression. If you choose to write with humor or sarcasm, make sure it's clear to the reader that that's what you're doing. The worst is when you're trying to be funny but your reader thinks you're being serious. Good natured sarcasm can be misinterpreted as bitterness and anger. If you decide to write in a flirtatious style, make sure you don't come across as cheesy or sleazy.

Content

Your goal is to convince the right man to contact you. That means you need to convey information in your essay that will appeal to him. If you want someone who travels, write about your travels and how you love seeing new places and experiencing new things. If you love helping people and want someone whom you can share that with, write about the volunteer work you do and the helping projects you are involved in. People connect with others who share common interests and goals. Put yours out there for likeminded partners to find.

Here's an example of a real profile sent to me by an attractive, 33 yr. old single woman. I'll explain why I think it's a winner after you've read it.

I've been making a bucket list before I even knew what a bucket list is. I see the glass half full and I thrive on change. I like the newness of things—it's not just being able to say I did things; it's the experience of it. That's why I moved to NYC. That's why I'm on jdate right now.

In the last few years, my bucket list brought me to Hawaii (on the list: "learn to surf"), to Florida ("learn how to fly a Cessna airplane"), to West Virginia ("rock climb 1,000 ft fin-rock"), and to the Whitney Museum ("visit the Whitney Museum") ha? 2011's list has a few good ones. Here's a little sample:-Learn Spanish. -See a NYC baseball/basketball game. I love cheering and being amongst the fans -Get my palm read. (I've never done it, and anyway, this city is full of readers. I'd like to go and see what she predicts, then laugh about it.)

I didn't just come to NYC for the experience, of course. I have my own company in Social Media Marketing and I love helping companies succeed. I am thankful all is well with work, despite the economy.

I'm the type of girl who can get dressed up in record time, hold my own at a cocktail party, and be spotted wearing jeans and a t-shirt the next day. I'm easy-going and have good values and a warm heart.

I've had some great relationships in the past with wonderful men that just didn't work for the long haul due to timing. C'est la vie...I'm hopeful and optimistic.

I have a fun talent: I can predict the end of movies. I was even pretty close on The Sixth Sense and Usual Suspects. Fight Club got me, though. It's a bummer of a skill, really. I think it's so much more fun to be surprised. What I'm saying here is: surprise me.

Let's analyze:

Paragraph 1: Her opening is fast paced and exciting. She tells you that she's positive, energetic, and open to new experiences. But she doesn't just come out and say these things. She does it subtly through images like "bucket list" and "glass half full". She's not ashamed to be on JDate. She's open and ready for a relationship.

Paragraph 2: She tells us about her travels and adventures, reinforcing her "not afraid of new experiences" opening. But there's another side to her too. She can enjoy being part of the crowd cheering on her team or getting her palm read. Before you label her a superstitious flake, she makes sure to clarify that she'll, "laugh about it". So she's fun *and* normal.

Paragraph 3 & 4: She informs us that she's a successful business woman, so men with low self esteem who can't handle that need not apply. Then she tells us that despite her success she's a down to earth, low maintenance, easy going, warmhearted gal. Yes, she's had relationships before that just haven't worked out, but not because she trashed them. Timing is everything. She's not bitter or jaded. She's ready to try again!

This woman conveyed who she is and what she's looking for in a smooth, exciting, and engaging manner. She didn't harp on any one point for too long and gave just enough information to peak the reader's interest without boring him.

I think the last paragraph is brilliant. She leaves us with a tease...a challenge. Surprise me. I dare you. Who's not going to want to take that challenge? Great profile.

Personal info

You don't need to reveal your deepest darkest secrets in your profile. You might not want to share those until later in the relationship. Ever hear the term – TMI – Too Much Information? Avoid TMI in your essays. You're not proposing marriage, you're just looking to go out on a date. You don't need to provide a list of medications, allergies, neuroses, or pet peeves in your essay. You don't need to discuss your dysfunctional family history or your toxic relationship with your boss. Save it. For now, just focus on getting the date!

Try to be open minded. I recently read a profile where a woman stated that she would never move from her current city. You mean to tell me that she would give up the love of her life and years of happiness to live in a specific city? I have to believe that when faced with that choice, she would choose love and happiness over location. So why place that obstacle in the way of true love right off the bat? Why not deal with it if it actually becomes an issue?

People love mystery. They are intrigued by the unknown. They crave gossip and secrets, the dirtier the better. Curiosity is one of the most powerful of human characteristics. It caused Adam and Eve to taste of the forbidden tree. If harnessed correctly, it could also whet the appetite of your potential mate. Don't give it all up in your essay. Leave your reader wanting to know more about you. Write something like, "I've traveled to some pretty exotic places, but describing them in person is so much more exciting...so I'll wait ;)" Intrigued?

Even if you follow my guidelines there's one important point to remember: not everyone is a good writer. There's nothing to be ashamed of. Everyone has different talents. If yours happens to be writing, you have a tremendous advantage in the profile writing category. Use it. If you're not a writer, don't give up hope. You can still write a coherent and interesting profile if you really put your mind, and some effort, into to it. Just keep it simple and to the point. If you try to be too fancy, funny, sophisticated, satirical, sardonic, sagacious, or sarcastic (or if you keep trying to use big words that basically reflect the same idea just to look cool) you will probably just succeed in motivating your reader to click and move on to the next profile.

There isn't anything dishonest or unethical about getting a professional to help you write your profile just like there's nothing wrong with having a professional photographer take your photos. Very few people will ask you out solely based on your writing style. It's more about the messages and information you convey and, of course, your photos.

Now it's time to get to work creating or modifying your online profile. I can't guarantee that if you follow my suggestions you'll suddenly get a flood of messages in your inbox. But I do believe that you'll significantly increase your chances of attracting the kind of man you're searching for.

Here are some guidelines to follow when writing your profile essays:

- ♥ Before you actually write anything, determine the message you want to send your reader?

- ♥ Don't confuse the reader with lots of irrelevant gibberish. Make sure you convey your message as clearly and concisely as possible within your chosen style.

- ♥ Don't reveal too much sensitive personal information. No need to scare anyone away just yet.

- ♥ Be honest.

- ♥ Be Positive.

- ♥ Write to attract the type of person you'd like to be with.

- ♥ Proofread before publishing. Check your grammar and spelling. Bad grammar and stupid spelling mistakes are a real turnoff for anyone with at least average intelligence.

- ♥ Always leave them wanting more.

Chapter Thirteen

Mixing Work and Pleasure

Only those who will risk going too far can possibly find out how far one can go.
— T. S. Eliot

Dating a coworker is risky business. It worked out great for Jim and Pam on The Office, but real life workplace romances don't usually end up so well. I can speak from personal experience. When the relationship is working, spending your work day in close proximity is amazing. When it's not, it's like being in hell and then some. If you work in a big company in different departments, and you don't see each other on a regular basis, then I don't see much of a problem, unless there's an explicit company rule against it. But if you do see each other or work together regularly, you need to tread with great care.

Don't think you can avoid the pitfalls by agreeing on rules of conduct to follow in the event of a breakup. Emotions trump rules every time. You might as well write those rules on a piece of toilet paper and insert them in the appropriate place. At least they will not have been a total waste. You'll probably never be able to return to the same coworker relationship you enjoyed before your romantic involvement. It might even get so unpleasant that you'll be forced to quit.

Now that I've sufficiently scared you from ever considering the possibility of dating a coworker, I'll offer you a ray of hope. Despite the dangers and pitfalls, in some cases I think it's worth the risk. If you truly believe, with all your heart, that this coworker who you've gotten to know so well is your *Bashert*, and if you're willing to bet your job on that, then go for it. True love is more important than any job, isn't it?

But you need to be as sure as you can possibly be that this man has the potential to go the distance with you. You're risking your livelihood here. Get to know as much about him as you can *before dating him*. Spend as much time with him as possible at work getting to know him *before dating him*. Isn't that what dating is all about anyway? So you're sort of dating him, without officially dating him. Let him know your fears about dating a coworker, so he's clear that you're taking this seriously. That will dissuade him from pursuing if all he's after is a quickie affair. If you do decide to date him, try to avoid getting sexually intimate until you feel secure in a committed relationship. If you subsequently break up and haven't yet had sex, the awkwardness and bad feelings will be a lot less than if you did. Think about it.

Your mission is to find your Mr. Right. Just because he works with you doesn't mean he's off limits. You just need to be extra careful and as sure as you can be that a relationship with this man has true potential. Remember, your livelihood might be at stake.

Chapter Fourteen

Timing Is Everything

If the timing's right and the gods are with you, something special happens.

— Rick Springfield

What if you've been targeting, networking, going to events, asking for help, looking online, and you still can't seem to find the man you're searching for? Are you doing something wrong? You might be. Before I try to help you figure out what you might need to modify, let's get a bit philosophical and talk about life.

There are two factors that will always remain beyond your control: timing and luck. A wise person once said, "timing is everything". It is the first commandment of dating. It trumps attraction, chemistry, and every other ingredient when starting a new relationship. If you meet the right person at the wrong time, you might as well have not met them at all. It would be a lot less painful.

You can probably look back at your own past relationships and imagine how different they might have turned out had you known then what you know now. But you were younger, less experienced, and less mature back then. You could try again now, but those guys are all married with kids.

Remember that guy David whom you met at that convention? You talked for hours. The chemistry was incredible and he was practically begging to date you, but you were already in a relationship. It was a bad relationship that was probably gonna end, but you weren't the type to cheat. As long as you were in a relationship, you were committed to seeing it through. A couple of months later you ran into David again and felt that same intense chemistry you did the first time around. This time you were single. You gathered up your courage and asked David out, telling him how you really had wanted to when you first met but you were seeing someone. He's flattered and impressed. He feels that chemistry too and would have been all over you a month ago. But, he's in a relationship now. Ouch, that hurts. A year later you run into David with his wife. Ok, enough torture. *Timing is everything.*

The other factor in finding your Mr. Right that is beyond your control is luck. Call it fate, *Mazel, bhadram,* it's all the same. Whatever you choose to call it, it's either there for you or not. There's nothing you can do to make it happen. Rabbits' feet, leprechauns, or knocking on wood won't do a darn thing (although many grandmothers will vehemently disagree). Luck is when you miss the bus to that exciting singles weekend only to meet a great guy who's in town to visit his sister who just happens to live next door to you. It's when you've sworn off all singles events but are convinced to go to just one more, and meet your soulmate there. Without a bit of luck you can do everything right but come away empty handed. The good news is that luck makes its way around to everyone, eventually. You just have to be ready, willing, and able to take advantage of it when it does present you with your golden opportunity.

You can easily blame your persistent single status on bad timing and bad luck, and continue doing what you're doing. You can also conclude that maybe there's something you can do or change to help you reach your objective. If you're willing to perform some self examination, here are some suggestions that you should at least consider.

Reevaluating your list

I know, you spent a lot of time developing, modifying, and redoing your I Do List. Maybe you need to re-evaluate it again to make sure that everything on it is realistic and achievable for you? After applying your list to real life dating situations you may have found that one or two items are just not as important or available as you originally thought. Or maybe they were realistic when you first wrote the list but now, a year or two later, they no longer fit your current reality?

One of the biggest mistakes that many women make is to hold on to their original lists without any modifications. A woman I know, Cheryl, was a hot ticket in her 20's and most of her 30's. Now she's in her 40's and still looking good, for her age. She always dated guys within a couple of years of her, on either side. Now things are a little more challenging. Most guys in their early to mid 40's want to date women in their 30's (sorry, but it's true). Lisa is still living in her 30's, searching for that successful thirty-something hunk to swoop down from his hedge fund trading desk and whisk her away to a romantic getaway at his Hampton's house (owned, no shares). Things aren't going so well for her (surprise) but her list still hasn't changed in a decade and a half. Unless she modifies it, she's going to remain in a cycle of frustration and unhappiness.

It's time to take a long hard look at that list and modify or delete items that you now realize are inapplicable or unrealistic, just like you did back in Chapter Two. I'm sure the list of foods that you liked as a five year old is very different from the foods you like today. As you grow, mature, and change, so too should your I Do List.

Remember the things we talked about in Chapters Five and Six, like appearance, attitude, and keeping an open mind? Are you staying fit, energetic, and positive? Are you looking your best? If you've answered no to any, some, or all of these questions, you need to put your butt into overdrive and get to work ASAP. Laziness is not an option. Do you want to find a man to spend the rest of your life with? Then stop making excuses and start making progress!

SECTION THREE

DATING 101

Chapter Fifteen

Whose Move Is It?

Love sought is good, but given unsought, is better.

— William Shakespeare

You did your research and discovered where your Mr. Right roams. Maybe you just lucked out (finally) and stumbled into the Mr. Right convention. You're excited. There are men in the room who appear to fit the important items on your I Do List. All you have to do now is meet them! How do you make that happen?

The first thing you need to do is verify that your target is single and available. If you're at a venue or event geared towards singles, you can assume (for now) that he is. If you're somewhere else, unless you're with a friend who knows him, you won't be able to verify his status. If you're worried about introducing yourself to a man who is already spoken for, don't be. If he's taken, he'll be flattered by your advance, and no harm done. He won't be angry, annoyed, or insulted. You'll feel proud that you had the "balls" to take the initiative and go after what you want. Bravo to you.

Women often roam in groups. Maybe it's a security thing. Men usually prowl alone. A group of happily chatting ladies can pose an intimidating scenario for a lone wolf trying to move in for the kill. He can handle a one on one, but one on three or more? He might find performing for an audience too difficult and move on to easier prey. If you want to get a man to come to you, you must break away from your wing-ladies and present him with a viable, easily approachable target. Hanging with your galpals might be fun, but it will stunt your chances of getting "hit on".

You want the man to approach you and make the first move. It confirms his interest and gives him the opportunity to be the hunter. Men enjoy the hunt almost as much as the actual "conquest". It gives them a huge adrenaline rush to remove any obstacles and do whatever it takes to win you over. If a man's interested, unless you're wearing a big sign that says keep away, he'll make a move. Some men won't even let the sign stop them. Full steam ahead!

There are a few possible reasons why a man won't make the first move.

- ♥ He hasn't noticed you.
- ♥ He's too shy or insecure to approach a goddess like you.
- ♥ He's not interested (hard to believe, I know).
- ♥ He's in a relationship or gay.

If he's in a relationship or gay, game over. Now let's analyze the other options. You might be giving off a vibe that's keeping this guy away. Some ladies sport an intense, almost angry, scowl on their face, regardless of their mood. That can scare off even the most confident fellow. I speak from experience. Most guys will just move on to easier pickings. You need to give off a positive, relaxed, and yes, happy, vibe if you want to lure that puppy dog into your lair. Here boy!

Sometimes, you won't be able to identify anything wrong with what you're doing. I've got a single female friend who is super attractive and sexy (that's my normal guy opinion). She's frustrated because she'll be sitting alone at a bar and not a single guy in a room full of them will approach her. And she smiles, gives off great energy, and even occasionally makes eye contact. Some of the guys check her out and smile at her, but for some reason, they don't have the "balls" to make a move. I don't know what to say. As a man I feel embarrassed for my fellow brothers. This girl is hot, and definitely not in a sleazy way. I seriously don't get it. All I can think of is that she's much too confident looking for the insecure and immature guys roaming the halls of Dating Game High.

Dating Alert

It's true, men can be extremely insecure. It doesn't matter how much weight they can lift or how much trash they can talk. Some of them are terrified of rejection. So, remember to be gentle.

If you've done your best to attract his attention and he still hasn't taken your bait, you've got two options: give up or go for it.

There are two schools of thought regarding women making the first move. The anti-movers claim that if a woman chases a guy or makes herself too easily available, he will get turned off. The pro-movers say that women should make their move whenever they please. I think both of these positions have merit.

The anti-movers are right in that a woman should never *chase* a man. When a guy is interested, he doesn't want to be chased. By taking away his hunting license, you're in a sense emasculating him. I don't think that's going to work too well for you. But making a move is not chasing. At least it shouldn't be. If you make your move correctly, you'll never be accused of chasing or even coming on strong.

Most women equate making a move with aggressive behavior. They think they have to come over and say something outrageously witty or cutesy or maybe even blatantly sexual to grab a guy's attention. But instead of dazzling the guy, they come across as aggressive, even desperate.

If a guy is interested it doesn't really matter what your opening line is and if he's not, it also doesn't matter. Remember that line from Jerry Maguire, "you had me at hello?" Well, hello is just about all you need to say to make your move on a guy. You can also say your name. That's about it. You don't need to say anything else. If you make your move with hello and your name, you're basically saying, "Here I am. If you're interested, YOU make the first move." You've brought the horse to water. Now it's his choice to drink or not. You're in no way being aggressive, and certainly not chasing or desperate. You're not really even making a move. You're just giving him the opportunity to do so. Ain't nothin' wrong with that. Men get an ego boost when they are approached by women. Even if they're not interested, they still feel all macho and big headed. So the worst you can do is boost a guy's confidence. Is that so bad?

If you do give him the opportunity and he doesn't act on it, move on. Don't try to make him interested by doing a stand up routine or song and dance number for him. You tried, and should be proud of that. Now it's time to confidently walk on by and on to the next one. But this is where many women unfortunately mess up. They continue to push themselves aggressively on a guy who has made his intentions clear. Don't make the same mistake. Let the guy make the first move. If he doesn't, give him the opportunity to by going over and saying hi. If he's interested, he'll take it from there.

Dating Alert

If you've decided to make your move and approach a guy, listen to what I'm about to say: first impressions last a very long time and are extremely hard to change. You get just one chance at a first impression, so make sure you look your best and are feeling positive and upbeat. If you just rolled out of bed with a nasty hangover and are wearing your old, baggy, velour sweatsuit, sneak away and come back to fight another day when you're better prepared for combat.

Chapter Sixteen

Dealing with the Competition

The healthiest competition occurs when average people win by putting above average effort.

— Colin Powell

The competition for good men is fierce. That's a fact. There are women out there competing for the same men as you are, who are younger and more beautiful than you. In some places, like NYC and LA, there are loads of them. If you're one of those beauties, you can probably stop reading this and continue doing whatever's been working for you. For the rest of you, I'd like to rid you of this problem once and for all. The way to handle competition in dating from ladies you don't think you can compete against is simple: don't compete.

Here are three tips for getting your man without competing against the unbeatable ones.

1. Don't Chase Model Chasers

You know the type and you know what they're after, yet you still try to grab their affection. What a waste of your time. So what if they're good looking, successful, and just plain smooth operators? When given the choice between you or that tall blonde creature with the huge eyes (and breasts), they will never choose you. Once you accept that, you'll be able to focus your attention on the men who you *can* get. These are the men who might not wear the All Star jerseys but can still hit the ball and get on base. They'll make you feel like a million bucks, if you give them the chance. Some of these guys might imagine themselves as model chasers, but the smart ones learn to accept their reality pretty quickly (after being blown off enough times) and focus on women who give them the time of day. That's where you sail in, wind in your hair, and not a model in sight.

2. Location, Location, Location

Remember that famous lyric from the Crosby, Stills and Nash song, "If you can't be with the one you love, love the one you're with". Well, when you're in a place where there is no competition, you command lots of attention. Your job is to find those places and use them as your private hunting reserves. If all the beautiful people are heading to the Hamptons, you stay in the city and feast on the leftovers. Don't get grossed out. There are plenty of high quality men that don't weekend in the hot spots and prefer to just hang close to home. This is your chance to pounce. Avoid the places where you know the competition is fierce. Pick your spots carefully and then dominate them.

3. Dominate Your Niche

If you were thinking of starting another online dating site, I'd tell you to forget it. You've got no chance against the big players like match.com and eharmony.com, who dominate the field. But if your plan is to start a dating site for underachieving lesbian athletes from Wisconsin with blue eyes and black hair, I'd say you've got a fighting chance of becoming the dominant player in the field. Apply this analogy to dating. Find your niche, the thing that differentiates you from the crowd, and be the best at that particular voodoo you do so well. You won't be able to compete against the all stars, but you will be able to attract those men who are into your particular *shtick*. For example, a man who's really into musicians might choose musical talent over model mania. A great sense of humor might trump a great set of breasts. Dominate your niche.

Going head to head against the runway superstars is social suicide. But what about the competition you can go up against, like all those women who aren't prettier, younger, or smarter than you? There are just so many of them everywhere, interfering with your chance to meet Mr. Right. The same rules that I mentioned above apply. You can compete in the dating game by not competing. Pick your location, choose your target, and give it your best shot.

Chapter Seventeen

Getting the Date

The Constitution only gives people the right to pursue happiness. You have to catch it yourself.

— Benjamin Franklin

One way or another, you're having your first conversation with your target guy. Now's your chance to turn a hot lead into a sale. Sorry for the business imagery, but you know what I mean. He's interested enough to take out his hunting gear and load his shotgun. But unless he fires, the hunt will turn into a friendly game of hide and seek, where you're left hiding while the other kids run off to a better game.

The good news is that before you even open your mouth, your odds of getting the date are about 90%. That's because he's attracted to you. If he wasn't, he wouldn't be chatting you up right now. And like it or not, attraction is the key factor for men in their decision to date or not to date. All you need to do is get him just another 10% further to cross the finish line. It's not very far to go, but if you fall short you lose.

A guy needs to be one hundred percent sure, at least at that moment of decision, to be able to "pop the question" and follow through. Yes, the follow through is key, but not at all guaranteed by the date request. I can see you're confused, even though you've had it happen to you many times. A guy will ask you out and then never call to make the date. I'll delve into that in the next chapter. For now, your goal is to make him interested enough to ask you out or take your info and promise to contact you. All you need is that extra 10%. But you can also lose percentage points pretty quickly and blow your opportunity completely.

Let me first tell you what not to do. Don't start sharing your whole life story with him. He doesn't want to hear it. Unless you were a Geisha in Tokyo for the last seven years and are anxious to continue honing your skills, save your story for when you're actually in a relationship. Then he'll either want to hear it or have no choice but to hear it. Don't start chatting away about the minutia of your uneventful day. He will run.

Feed his hunger for challenge and his dreams of conquest by creating an aura of mystery and excitement around yourself. Give him just enough information to get his imagination working overtime. A few well placed sentences, pauses, smiles, and "I can't really talk about that now" will be more than enough to get the date. Less is more in the art of seduction.

Let's go through an example. Don has come over and introduced himself. You're in love. He asks you what your favorite travel destination is. You say Paris.

"Why is that?" he asks.

"I went there last summer and loved it," you reply.

"What did you do that was so great?" he asks.

"I can't really talk about that now," you answer, a soft smile spreading across your slightly blushing face. "But it was an experience I'll never forget," you add, with a mischievous twinkle in your eye.

What do you think is rushing through Don's mind at this point? He wants to jump you right then and there. Instead of reviewing your entire ten day itinerary or which museums you liked best, you have planted the seeds of mystery and excitement in his fertile imagination with a phrase, a blush, and a twinkle. Game on!

Another way of boosting your odds at getting the date takes a lot less creativity, but could ignite his imagination just the same: a light touch. Research has shown that elbow touching waitresses made 36% more in tips from male customers than non touching waitresses. I wonder why? Because that little touch is like throwing a lighted match into a barrel of gasoline. Don't make it obvious or sexual. Just relaxed and nonchalant. He won't miss it.

In most cases you shouldn't spend more than a few minutes talking with your target. All you want to do is get him interested. That doesn't take long. Then say you'd love to talk more but you really have to leave to meet some friends. If you've done your job, he'll pop the question. You're leaving him wanting more, which is the only way you want to leave a stage. You've given him a preview, now make him pay to see the whole show. As much as you want to continue hanging out with him right there and then, you must leave him wanting more. He needs to commit to a date to enjoy more of your company. You're worth that much, aren't you? Don't sell yourself short.

The only exception is if you've forged one of those deep and meaningful connections that most people just dream about. If you've hit that jackpot you can put in the hours, on one condition. You need to make sure that he is clearly available and is treating your encounter as a prelude to a relationship and not just some friendly rap session. How do you do that? Read the next chapter to find out.

Chapter Eighteen

Is He Out of Your League?

Once we accept our limits, we go beyond them.

— Albert Einstein

A lot of words have been written about men trying to date women they consider to be out of their league. Well what about a woman who wants to date a man she feels is out of her league? Should you even try?

Before we get to my answer, let's really understand the question. What does "out of your league" really mean? Is there a secret book of rules and regulations that dictates a strict caste-like system of dating hierarchies in which you can only date men who belong to a specific level of membership? Most people create their own list of requirements to follow, which is their choice, but there are no standardized requirements I know of that define what league you're playing in and who you can and cannot play with. Whether someone is or is not "in your league" is a barrier that you create in your mind that prevents you from taking chances and protects you from potential rejection.

I'm not going to tell you that every man will want to date you. You already know that. But just because a man fits a certain stereotype of someone who doesn't date women like *you*, doesn't mean he actually is that man. For example, just because a man is incredibly handsome doesn't mean he won't date a woman who isn't as good looking as he is. Sure, that might be the case, but I've seen plenty of cases where it wasn't. The only way you'll find out is if you give it a shot and go for it. Let him know you're interested and see what happens.

If you decide to take a chance and make the first move with a man you consider to be "out of your league" there's one thing you must possess to have a shot at success: Confidence. Confidence radiates and makes you shine. It transforms average looking women (and men) into super attractive and desirable dating partners. A confident lady sends out signals that draw a man to her. Without confidence you might as well stay home and watch TV, because you won't be able to catch much more than a bad cold, definitely not the kind of man you want to date.

Let me be clear. I'm not telling you that if you radiate confidence you will get the man whom you consider to be "out of your league". But without it, you definitely do not have a prayer.

So is he out of your league? No such thing.

Should you give it a shot and go for it? Yes, but only if you display confidence in yourself.

Will he say yes? Maybe. Go ahead and try. You've got nothing to lose except for a bruised ego. Are you gonna let that stop you?

Chapter Nineteen

Prelude to a Date

The trust of the innocent is the liar's most useful tool.

— Stephen King

Before you get involved with a man, you need to make sure he's available. "But if he's not available, why would he flirt with me or want to date me?" she naively asked. Welcome to the real world. Most men are honest and upstanding members of civilized society who will not mislead you into thinking that they are available when they're not. Unfortunately, there are more than a few who are bent on getting what they want without giving a hoot about how they might affect anyone else, including you.

      Online dating sites are fertile breeding ground for men looking for some cheating love. Among their millions of authentically single male users are thousands of married men in search of pretty young gals like yourself to flirt with, date, and hook up with. All they have to do is click the "single" box in their relationship status and, game on. If there are sites that check users marital statuses, I'm unaware of them. I know the popular ones don't. They should.

Meeting someone in person, the old fashioned way, is not necessarily much safer. Lots of married men don't wear wedding rings. Even if they do, it's not hard to remove a ring before entering a bar. If a man is engaged or in a serious relationship, there's no way to know without him telling you.

When you meet someone in a social situation it's usually pretty easy to determine if he's married by asking basic questions like where he lives, where he works, and where he usually hangs out. These are all pieces of information that you can use to get a feel for someone. Secret Married Guy doesn't want you to know anything about his real life, because that could lead to trouble when you pop over to visit him and meet his wife at the door. If he avoids your questions or seems awkward and evasive when answering, you need to go on alert and dig deeper. You can often tell if someone's lying by his body language. Does he look nervous, is he avoiding your eyes, is he shifting uncomfortably?

If you're not good at interrogations or judging body language, don't despair. If you've met this guy in a social situation, chances are you have mutual friends whom you can ask about him. If not, you can Google him for free, or search for his info on a paid database records site. If he's got his arm around a woman on his Facebook page, you should make further inquires. If he's in a tux and she's in a wedding gown, run.

If you're suspicious and can't find any evidence, you've got one option left. Look him straight in the eye and ask. That way there's no room for misunderstanding. Are you in a relationship?

Married? Yes or no. I don't see anything wrong with asking, and I can't see why any guy would hold it against you.

You can find a way to ask the question in a funny way to avoid any awkwardness, as long as you make sure he understands that it's a serious question requiring a serious answer. I know so many women who would have saved so much time, aggravation, and heartache if they had just bothered to ask if the guy was taken. They just didn't think that a guy would want to get involved unless he was available. Now they know better, I hope.

Here's a true real life scenario that happens quite often. Sarah was taking a course with a guy she hadn't seen for years. He told her that he recently moved to NYC and would love to get together and catch up. He was quite friendly to her. They spent some time chatting and exchanging texts. He was really anxious to hang out. He asked if she'd like to have dinner with him after class. Ok, sure. At dinner he mentioned that he regularly traveled to his hometown. Interesting.

"Why?" she asked, curiously.

"To see my girlfriend," he replied, innocently, a smug grin plastered across his face.

They split the check and Sarah left dazed, confused and pretty pissed off. Why didn't he mention anything about a girlfriend during any of their previous communications (flirtations)?

Let's not lynch this dude just yet. Let's give him the benefit of the doubt. He really did just want to catch up on old times, with absolutely no intention of misleading Sarah into thinking that he was single and available. But isn't it strange that his girlfriend didn't come up in conversation? Ok, let's say she just didn't, and he didn't think anything of it. He was just being friendly, with not the slightest intention of flirting with this attractive girl or exploring a bit further? Hmmm. Let's just say all this is true (you need to stretch your imagine here). The verdict in this case: GUILTY. If he's flirting with you, he needs to let you know he's UNAVAILABLE ASAP, not during what appears to be a date. Maybe there should be a ring that single men (and women) are forced to wear signifying that they are in an exclusive relationship. That would solve everything.

No matter how diligent you are in asking and researching, if you're dealing with a particularly unscrupulous individual who is determined to do whatever it takes to have his affair to remember, he will be able to fool you. If he's careful with his online photos and false information, there's little you can do to uncover his evil designs, at least initially. But after a bit of time you should be able to notice things that just don't seem kosher.

Here are some examples:

♥ **He never takes you to his home.**
Most single guys dream of getting you back to their place for a "nightcap". They'll do whatever it takes to make it happen. If your guy isn't, there's something fishy.

♥ **He doesn't introduce you to his friends.**
Guys love showing off their good looking dates. It's a boost to their macho man ego. If your guy is hiding you, there's a problem.

♥ **He only takes you to out of the way places.**
Refer to previous entry. Sometimes out of the way places are cool. Not all the time.

- ♥ *He doesn't take you to popular venues or events where he might know people.*

  More blatant than the previous entry. There are certain events that everyone attends. Why isn't he taking you?

- ♥ *He doesn't have a home number.*

  Fair enough, not everyone has a home phone anymore. But does he have two cellphones, and you only have his work number?

- ♥ *He can never see you on weekends or holidays.*

  These are the times made for dating. What is he up to?

If you feel you're costarring in a spy thriller, you know there's something wrong. Demand to see his home on a Sunday morning. Make him take you to the most popular restaurant in his town on the night before Thanksgiving. Spend New Year's Eve together. Trust your instincts and get the answers you need. If you still don't feel comfortable, get out. Under no circumstances are you allowed to become "the other woman". You will ruin your life and his. You deserve better.

Chapter Twenty

Finally, the Date

In the end, you're measured not by how much you undertake but by what you finally accomplish.

— Donald Trump

He took your contact info and called you. Hurray! Why am I so excited that a guy did what he said he would do? Because at least half of the guys out there don't. They'll take your number and file it for use in the event of total nuclear apocalypse. So why did they bother taking it in the first place? Because they felt like it in the moment. I could give you a laundry list of possible reasons that'll add another few pages to this book, but it'll just waste your time and mess with your head. The only right answer to why he didn't follow through on his pledge is that it just doesn't matter. He's history. Move on.

But he did call, so it should be smooth sailing at least until the actual date. Not so fast. Some dates don't make it past the first phone call. This applies primarily to blind dates, where the first phone call is your first contact with this stranger. You've both committed to meeting but are still not sure what to expect. You're trusting your friend or matchmaker, but you're understandably nervous. The phone call is your only chance to screen this guy and bail if necessary. He's thinking the same thing. In most cases the call will go just fine. He'll keep it short, ask you out, make the date, tell you where to meet, and done. Unfortunately, not all guys can carry out that simple sequence of tasks. Here are some things that could go wrong:

He says things that are so weird, freaky, insulting, or just plain stupid that you can't help but hang up, shower, and change your number. This happened to a woman I set up with a guy I know. He's a really nice guy, but instead of just asking her out on the phone he got into this whole conversation that went very wrong and made him sound like a stupid jerk. She refused to go out with him. I don't blame her.

He's so indecisive that he can't decide on a venue for the date. Some women aren't bothered by this and are happy to offer a suggestion. Others find this indecisiveness really unattractive and emasculating. Your choice.

He chats with you for a while and then doesn't ask you out. Maybe he didn't like the sound of your voice? Next!

Another potential stumbling block to a first date is phone tag. We've all been caught in an annoying game of phone tag. It's hard not to. But you don't want it to ruin a potential relationship. Here are some ways to avoid the problem:

If you're expecting the guy to call, try to answer your phone even though you don't recognize the number. With all the spam calls out there that could get really annoying, but take the pain and avoid the game.

If he calls and leaves a voice mail, unless he specifically says that he will call you back, call him back as soon as possible. If he says he'll call you back or if you leave him a voicemail, make sure you answer his call no matter what. Now that you've got his number on your caller ID, you've got no excuse. If you're in a meeting at work, step out for a minute (if at all possible) and take the call. You can also tell him what the best time is when he can reach you, when you leave your voicemail.

The longer the phone tag continues, the higher the chance is that either you or he will get frustrated and give up. To avoid all of the potential drama some matchmakers will actually plan the first date and just tell the man and woman the time and place. Not a bad idea.

Fast forward. You're going on your first date with a new guy. Now it's time to relax and enjoy. That's the primary purpose of a first date. You don't need to interview the guy to make sure he's Mr. Right. You've got a bit of time for that. Just see if you can get along and have a nice time together. Of course, you should always keep your eyes and ears open for obvious red flags (see Chapter 24). You can also start gathering basic information about the guy like family, work, and general likes and dislikes. But try to keep it light and relaxed.

Be yourself. I know that's a scary thought, because you've got so many things about you that you're not totally satisfied with and wish you could change. But your mission here is to find a man whom you can spend the rest of your life with, and unless you plan on becoming a different person, you need him to like *you*, the real you, just the way you are right here and now.

But let's say you're really crazy about this guy. You think he could really be the one. You want to do everything you can to win him over. You interrogate mutual friends, scour the internet, and tail him for a couple of days, to find out everything you can about him. You discover that he's a diehard conservative, loves country music, baseball, red meat, and his favorite movies are Jack Ass 1, 2, and 3. You, on the other hand, are a bleeding heart liberal vegetarian who loves opera, tennis, and black and white Hollywood classics. To hell with your list, you want this guy, period. So you wear your closest thing to a cowgirl outfit, praise George W. and Kenny Rogers, pledge allegiance to the Yankees, and surprise him with tickets to The Hangover III.

Your little charade succeeds. He digs you, big time. Feels an incredible connection. Can't wait to take you home to meet Mamma on the ranch. Now what? Are you prepared to spend the rest of your life acting out your new role? I didn't think so. So all you've accomplished is to waste his time and yours and possibly cause him, and yourself, unnecessary heartache and anger when he finds out who you really are. Would you like someone to do that to you?

Your goal is to find a partner who fits who YOU are, who appreciates YOU for who YOU are NOW. Don't try to fool anyone, because in the end, you'll be the fool.

When you got past Chapter One of this book, you made the decision to be a serious dater. Now's your chance to put your decision into practice. Most first dates are last dates. Sometimes the reasons are obvious. You felt like throwing up every time you looked at him. You were disgusted by his graphic usage of a broad array of words and phrases commonly found in pornographic literature (from what I hear). Most of the time it's not as clear cut. You might not have seen any fireworks or gotten chills down your spine, but it wasn't that bad either. It's in cases like these that a serious dater will give the guy another shot to prove himself.

I'm not telling you to go out on a second date with every guy you date. I'm no sadist. Just keep an open mind. Not everything about the guy needs to be exactly as you envisioned in your last daydreaming session. Remember, you're looking for potential, not perfection. In most cases a man can be polished up a bit to your liking. I'm not talking about core values and character traits. I'm talking about superficial things like clothing and etiquette.

Two women I know come to mind here. I tried to set each of them up with guys I knew. Both of these guys were successful, personable, and decent looking. Unfortunately, their sense of fashion was a bit lacking. It didn't bother them. Heck, they probably had no idea they were doing anything wrong. But to each of these women their lack of fashion style reflected on their character. One woman remarked, "he's just not sharp." So they passed and moved on, and are still passing and moving on in their casual dating way.

A serious dater would have recognized that clothing cluelessness is something easily corrected, at the right time, in the right way. Most men would love to have their clothing laid out for them by a woman with good fashion taste. It makes life that much easier. Do you have an issue with doing a bit more shopping?

REMEMBER

- ♥ Keep an open mind and look for potential, not perfection.
- ♥ Give your date the benefit of the doubt.
- ♥ If he's said or done something that you consider to be "wrong", don't convict him right away. Maybe he had a bad day? Maybe you misunderstood what he meant or did? Maybe it was just a onetime thoughtless mistake? Cut him some slack.
- ♥ Give it one more chance.
- ♥ Don't give up on someone after one bad date. If you felt an initial attraction, then you MUST give it at least another shot, maybe even two -- unless there's a really compelling reason not to (like the guy turns out to be a psycho). I always hear married women saying that the first time they met their husbands they weren't the least bit interested, but they saw some potential so they gave it another shot. The rest is history.
- ♥ First dates can be awkward. That's why you should go out on a second date whenever possible.

Chapter Twenty-One

Put Down That Phone!

For love would be love of the wrong thing; there is yet faith, But the faith and the love and the hope are all in the waiting.

— T. S. Eliot

Date one was a success. You didn't drool, throw up, or get drunk and make an ass out of yourself. The conversation flowed, you had stuff in common, and surprisingly, you had fun. You can't wait for him to ask you out again. But you must. You must wait for him to contact you. Put down that phone! If you like you can send him a text that says, "Had a really nice time. Thanks!" But that's it. Just one line, short, sweet, and to the point. You've passed him the ball confidently and securely. It's his move.

You wait. Under no circumstances should you contact him again until he first contacts you. I don't care if you just got the last two box seat tickets to game seven of the World Series. You wait. If you feel you just cannot stop yourself, call me and I will come over immediately and confiscate your phone and smash your modem. Am I making myself clear?

If a guy wants to ask you out again, he will. It's really as simple as that. If he's super busy at work, or traveling in Africa, or in bed with the flu, he'll find two minutes to call, text, email or send a homing pigeon. If he loses your number he will find it. If he can't he will go to your house and ask you in person. He will find you and ask you. Until he does, do not contact him. If he doesn't contact you within a few days, assume that he's not interested and go out with the next guy on your list. If he contacts you later with a valid excuse, you can always go out with him again if you still want to.

I can tell you're fighting me on this. You're saying, "I'm a modern, confident, independent woman. Why can't I take charge of the situation and call him?" Because you have absolutely nothing to gain from doing so. He's either interested or not. If he is, he would have called. If he's not, do you think your call is going to change his mind? If he wasn't interested in you enough to call you after the first date, why do you think things will be different now? Maybe if the first date was really off due to some extraordinary circumstances, a normal second date might turn out differently? Could be. But if your initial date was fine and you enjoyed it, what can possibly change that will suddenly make him interested? Nothing.

If you do break my rule and call him and he accepts your offer to get together again, beware. The reason he's accepting is because he figures he can get some easy action, of the carnal variety. You've shown him that you're really hot for him. You're chasing him. So why not have some fun, make you happy, and then blow you off again? You are what they call "easy pickings". If that works for you, by all means call him right now. But if you're serious about getting into a relationship that leads to marriage, wait for him to contact you.

Chapter Twenty-Two

Why Didn't You Get a Second Date?

Success consists of going from failure to failure without loss of enthusiasm.
— Winston Churchill

Rejection is part of the dating process. It happens to everyone. Why didn't you get a second date, even though your first date seemed to go so well? The only way to know for sure is to hear your rejecter's reason. That rarely happens. To be accurate, you might get a reason, but it's almost never the truth. No guy is going to tell you to your face that he hated your look, got nauseous from your pungent breath, or would rather have jumped out a window than continue listening to another boring story. You'll probably hear something like, "there just wasn't any chemistry", or "it just didn't feel right". You can fill in your excuse of choice.

So why didn't you get a second date when you thought that the first date went relatively well, maybe even very well? What did you do wrong? Probably nothing. Ever hear the infamous phrase, "It's not you, it's me"? Even though it sounds like a nice way to hide the real, sinister, reason, it's usually the plain simple truth. The fact that a guy with whom you spent a pleasant evening doesn't want to spend another with you usually has absolutely nothing to do with you. For whatever reason (which is frankly none of your business), he's decided that he just doesn't want to see you again, period. Maybe you don't fit his image of ideal beauty or maybe you're too attractive or smart or personable and he just can't handle it? It could be anything, and at the end of the day, it just doesn't matter because, "it's not you, it's him".

Feel better? Not so fast. Sometimes the reason why you didn't get a second date is totally your fault, and if you had done things differently, you'd be getting that second date. Here are some possibilities:

You Looked Like Hell

There are some women who look great under any circumstances. They can roll out of bed, throw on a potato sack, and walk out into a drenching downpour, and the guys will come flocking. You've seen some of these ladies on the big screen. If you are one of them, you probably can skip this chapter. Otherwise, listen up. When you're on a date, or in any social situation, you need to look your best. For some ladies that means spending hours applying makeup, picking out clothing and conferring with friends. For others it's a painless twenty minute process. Whatever it means for you, do it. Don't get lazy and say, "if he doesn't like the real me, as is, that's his problem." It's your problem if you like him and he doesn't want to see you again because you looked like an extra on the set of Night of the Living Dead.

You Pissed Him Off

There was an episode on a TV show about dating where the woman had a great first date and the guy didn't contact her for a week or so after. He finally did text her to ask her out and she accepted, despite her extreme frustration about him not contacting her sooner. On the date she felt that she couldn't put aside her ruffled feathers, so she told the guy that she felt upset that he had waited so long to contact her again. That really ticked him off. He felt that she was unreasonable and much too high maintenance. The rest of the date seemed to go well, and he actually did set up a third date, in order to break up with her in person.

Regardless of how hot a woman is, and she was pretty hot, there's a point at which a guy will just decide she's not worth the trouble and aggravation. It might happen after a first date, or maybe not until after the fifth. I'm not telling you to walk on eggshells and be afraid to speak your mind. Just think before you say anything that might rub your date the wrong way.

You Didn't Shut Up For a Minute

In his classic book *How To Win Friends and Influence People*, Dale Carnegie observed that people love listening to their own voice and if you give them that opportunity, they will feel like they had a great conversation with you, even if you barely spoke. Those are wise words.

There's nothing wrong with talking and sharing. That's what conversation is all about. But there's also nothing wrong with asking your date questions to show that you're genuinely interested in what he has to say, and most importantly, listening. If you talked the entire time without giving your date the chance to get in a word edgewise, you probably came home feeling like you had the best conversation ever. Your date probably felt otherwise.

You Were a Bitch

You made and took personal calls and texted throughout the date. You were rude to everyone around you, including your date. You belittled his profession, education, and just about everything else about him. Need I say more?

It doesn't really matter why he didn't ask you out again. He didn't. Don't waste time overanalyzing, complaining, feeling down, and acting as if he was the last guy on earth and you'll be spending your life alone and miserable. You're on a mission and you're not gonna let some shmo throw you off track. Get positive, get confident, and get back out there and find your Mr. Right.

Your date agenda should include:

- ❤ Looking your best
- ❤ Emitting positive energy
- ❤ Asking your date about what he does professionally and for fun.
- ❤ Listening attentively to his responses like you really care.
- ❤ Being nice to him, and everyone else you interact with.
- ❤ Not texting, emailing, or making or taking calls.
- ❤ Focusing on the date.

Chapter Twenty-Three

———♡♡♡———

You Gotta Know When to Hold 'Em

Adopt the pace of nature: her secret is patience.

— Ralph Waldo Emerson

You've made it past the first date or two. Now the goal is to transform dating into relationship. That's when you no longer need to worry if you're going to see him again, and when you are the ONLY woman he's seeing (and he's the only man you're seeing). In order to get from dating to relationship you need to heed the advice I'm about to give you in this chapter.

A friend of mind recently set up a mutual female friend with a buddy of his from work. She's very attractive, mid 30's, sweet, athletic, and fun to be with. She was crazy about the guy. He broke up with her after a month. He said that she was too available. There was no challenge. He said, "when I went away to Florida for a week, she texted me about ten times every day!"

My first reaction to this story was that he obviously isn't ready to get married because if he was, he would be thrilled to have this amazing woman so head over heels in love with him. Then I thought about it a little more and started getting mysteriously claustrophobic and freaked out, like I was standing in for Michael Douglas in Fatal Attraction.

Ladies, let's pull out the male operating manual. It takes the average guy longer to become emotionally attached to a woman than vice versa. Initially, he focuses primarily on a woman's outer beauty and the sexual attraction he feels for her. It could take weeks before he begins to develop a deeper emotional connection.

In this initial stage a significant part of that sexual attraction a guy feels is based on the challenge of winning you over. He is in hunter mode, adrenaline pumping, testosterone at super high levels, totally focused on one objective: to make you his own (use your imagination). Your primary mission is to keep him in this state of pursuit for as long as possible, until he has a chance to form an emotional connection with you. The longer you keep the chase going, the better your chances of forming a true and lasting relationship.

Women often ask, "If a guy tries to hook up with you right away - is he not taking you seriously?"

He's doing what he's instinctively trained to do. Whether he's serious or not is irrelevant. His brain isn't doing a lot of thinking at this point. His penis is running the show. You have the prize he desperately wants to possess. He will say and do practically anything to win that prize. He will stay in the game until he gets it. The longer you keep the game going, the better your chances of winning; i.e. forming a lasting relationship.

Some women think that if they don't surrender the prize right away, the guy will move on to easier prey. So they give up the prize and end up losing the guy anyway. This is a huge mistake. If you are looking for a lasting relationship, then any guy who will leave if he doesn't get his prize when he wants it is NOT the guy for you. He's not the man you want to walk down the aisle with and be the future father of your children. Think about it.

Now let's discuss communication. You really want to check in with your new guy friend at least five times a day and have long phone conversations before bed every night. You want him to show that he cares about you by calling, sending romantic texts and emails, and making you the center of his life. You have every right to want that, but you'll send him running in the process.

Guys need their space. They don't feel the need to check in with you at all during the day, unless they have something important to tell you. Many guys don't like talking on the phone for too long in any case. Their idea of communication is much more functional than yours. If they have nothing they need to say, they would rather skip the conversation, say a quick goodnight, and go on with their business. This doesn't mean that you can't communicate with him at all. One text a day is plenty. Let him take charge and be a hunter. Let him chase *you*.

I know you want to spend as much time with him as possible to build your relationship. You are right to want that. But remember that he is the hunter and needs the challenge. He needs to be the one to court you. If he isn't making the effort to spend as much time with you as you would like, don't get frustrated. Just do your own thing. Live your life. If he calls and you've already made plans, too bad for him. Let him know you'd really love to see him but you need more than a few hours notice to plan your schedule. Show him that you have a life. It won't turn him off. It'll just make him want you more. It might be frustrating initially, but in the long run, you will be happy you weren't so "available".

I hate games, and I wish you didn't have to play them, but in the reality of today's dating scene, sometimes you do. Holding back is the most powerful tool in your arsenal. Use it wisely and you'll greatly increase your chances of creating a lasting relationship with the right man.

Chapter Twenty-Four

Is He Serious About This?

Nothing is worth doing unless the consequences may be serious.

— George Bernard Shaw

You're on a mission and don't want to waste anymore time, so you want to make sure that this man you've started dating is serious about entering into a relationship that will lead to marriage. You can never know for sure, even if you ask. All you can do is make it clear to him what you're looking for in a relationship, and hope he gets the message.

Will you scare him off if you tell him early on that you're looking for a serious relationship that might lead to marriage? If you do, he's obviously not ready to make that kind of commitment. You're not asking him to marry you now or ever. All you want to know is if he is *ready* to be in a committed relationship that may *eventually* lead to marriage. That should only scare off the guys who are just interested in tasting, not buying. If marriage is not even on his longer term radar screen, you want to pinch his cheek and send him off before you get involved in something you'll regret.

The only way to build a relationship is to spend quality time together. If the guy you've started dating can't find the time, he's probably not interested in being in a committed relationship or is just plain clueless. There might be some total knuckleheads out there who just don't understand the whole dating and relationship thing and think they can dabble in it at their leisure. Most guys get it. If they're not doing it, they're not interested.

Signs that he's not interested:

- ♥ He regularly texts you a couple of hours before the weekend to see if you want to hang out later that night.
- ♥ He'll contact you to meet on very short notice. You tell him you're busy. He doesn't contact again for a while. Repeat sequence.
- ♥ He only sends you brief texts. He never has long phone conversations with you.
- ♥ He hangs out with his close friends, and never asks you to join.
- ♥ He only wants to see you for late night booty calls.
- ♥ He's not interested in learning more about you.
- ♥ He's always too busy to find the time to see you.

Some guys are experts at keeping you hanging while they live their lives to the fullest. They like you but not enough to commit, so they send you occasional flirtatious texts and meet up once in a while, when it's convenient for them. It takes two to play this game. If you stop, game over. If you ignore his flirtatious texts or respond with one or two word answers, he'll realize that you're not playing and decided to either get serious or get out. If you happen to be busy when he calls you to meet up in an hour, he'll get the same message. If he wants to date you, be attentive and available. If he wants to play with you, no thanks. You don't play with boys.

Contrary to the popular theory of, "He's Just Not That Into You", the fact that he's not interested in a relationship with you doesn't mean he doesn't like you or isn't attracted to you. It just means he's not ready or willing to have a relationship with you. Maybe it's because he doesn't think you fit his I Do List, or maybe it's because he doesn't want a serious relationship with anyone at the moment. Do you really care?

If he's interested in a relationship with you he'll make time to see you, plan ahead to make sure you're available, call you to talk and get to know you, and proudly introduce you to his close friends. It's so clear and obvious, yet so many women still haven't gotten it. They see the signs but get all confused and frustrated, instead of getting smart and moving on.

I don't mean to imply that moving on is easy. It might have been a long time since you met someone you felt a connection to and you want to do everything possible to build on that initial spark. Your imagination has been working overtime constructing romantic scenarios with your new Prince Charming. You're crazy about him.

It's hard to just walk away from something that seems so right. But you must, because he already has. If he shared your vision he'd be banging down your front door at this very moment.

Take control of your life. Send those playboys packing and date only those guys who show you they are serious.

Chapter Twenty-Five

When to Throw In the Towel

Part of being a winner is knowing when enough is enough. Sometimes you have to give up the fight and walk away, and move on to something that's more productive.

— Donald Trump

How many dates should you go on before throwing in the towel if you just don't feel it's right? This is a tough one to answer because every situation is different. It depends on what's making you not "feel right".

Let's say you're not physically attracted to the guy, but you really like his personality and enjoy spending time with him. According to most of women I speak to, that's pretty much the story of at least one of their serious relationships. In fact, many of these women are married to the guys they didn't initially have the hots for. If you are, or think you could be, part of that group, I recommend that you go out with the guy a few more times and see what develops. If nothing does, at least you know you did your best to make it work. You're not leading him on by giving him a chance to light your fire. He should be thanking you. If he's not, well, that's his problem. You're innocent.

If the level of attraction you're seeking is of the big screen variety, where you are overwhelmed by a desire to rip off his clothing and make wild and crazy "love" to him all the time, everywhere, you might wait a long time and end up disappointed and alone. That doesn't mean you shouldn't strive for it. It just means you shouldn't make it a requirement on your I Do List, and pass on guys who don't meet it. This type of attraction could develop months into a relationship, but you'll never know if you don't give it a chance.

Let's say you are physically attracted to him and you have fun together. You continue dating him, right? Yes, but with one caveat. If you know for sure that he doesn't meet one of your must have I Do List items without which you know you can never be happy, you must break it off. If you can change your expectations or requirements, great. But don't expect him to change down the road.

I'm not referring to superficial attributes like weight, manners, and clothing style. These things can, and do, change with the right support and effort. Some things don't, or at least cannot be expected to, change. Here are a few:

Personality

If he's serious and "heavy" all the time, he's not going to suddenly become lighthearted and carefree. If he's stingy, he probably won't become the guy who picks up the check for the table. If he's lazy, don't expect Mr. Ambitious. If he's nasty and mean, don't even think about it.

Family

If you have serious issues with his family, there's not a whole heck of a lot he can do to change where he comes from. He could choose to distance himself from them, but do you really want to be the obstacle between a man and his family? He'll never forgive you.

Life Goals

We discussed this when you created your I Do List. If his life goals contradict yours, unless you're willing to change yours, you need to call it quits. Some life goals can be discussed and compromised on. Some are just too powerful. You should try to determine what those are for him as soon as possible. If you see that there's an irreconcilable clash, take the cue and exit the relationship.

Mental Health Issues

Whether you continue seeing a man with mental health issues is a decision that only you can make. Many conditions including depression, bipolar disorder, and OCD can be successfully treated through medication and psychotherapy. Treatments affect individuals differently. There are no cures. If you do decide to continue in the relationship, be prepared to deal with the issue throughout your life together.

Abusive Behavior

If you detect abusive behavior directed at you or at anyone else, you should stop dating him and move on. Nobody deserves to be abused.

Don't try to be the one who's going to save him from himself. There are professionals who are trained to help. If he uses them and you see genuine change, you can give him another chance. Otherwise, out.

I realize that the items I just listed are obvious, but sometimes even the best of us can be blinded by attraction and infatuation. You've all heard the quintessential tale of the woman who falls for the tall, handsome, filthy rich doctor (you can fill in your own profession) who wines, dines, and romances her. She is in love. Then the abuse starts. It's primarily verbal, although sometimes gets a bit physical, but nothing too bad. She obviously isn't happy about it, but she's willing to cut him some slack and forgive and forget, as long as she can have the lifestyle she's always dreamt of. She marries him. The abuse gets worse. Or maybe it's not abuse. Maybe it's irreconcilable life issues, severe depression, or an unbearably intrusive family. You can finish the story yourself. It usually doesn't end well.

If you determine that the man you've started dating is definitely not going to work for you, you need to do the right thing for you and for him and break it off. It's the right thing for him because you don't want to lead him on. It's even more important for you because if you continue dating him you might end up falling for him despite your reservations. Then you'll be faced with the same decision, only it'll be infinitely harder and more painful. Or worse, you'll marry him.

In the event that you like the man you're dating and there are no major red flags that you can see, you should continue dating him and cut him a lot of slack. That means ignoring lots of little things that might at times annoy you. You aren't perfect either. I remember an episode of Seinfeld where Jerry is dating a woman who seems perfect except that she eats her peas one by one. Then there's the beautiful woman who has "man hands". Or the one who's very perfection is what annoys him. Jerry breaks up with all of them. He's just not interested in getting married. But you are, so you better learn how to ignore the insignificant stuff or face playing trivial pursuit for a very long time.

If I had dated my wife ten years earlier I probably would have broken up with her after a few dates (she probably would have beat me to it). That's because ten years earlier I wasn't focused on getting married so every tiny thing that I didn't love would be sufficient grounds for breaking up. I was focused on perfection. Anything you do or say can and will be held against you, I proclaimed. Who could possibly run that gauntlet and survive?

Ten years older and wiser I entered each date with the attitude of, "unless you give me a really good reason to leave, I'm going to do everything in my power to make this work." With that attitude I was able to let the stupid stuff slide and focus on the important things. It worked for me, and I think it will for you too.

If your goal is committed relationship or marriage, you should not continue in a relationship for more than three months without knowing for sure that the man you're dating shares the same objective. He doesn't need to know if he wants to marry you. He just needs to want to get married in the not too distant future. Ideally you want to know this piece of information as soon after beginning to date him as possible, the sooner the better. But three months is the break point when you either know the man has serious intentions or is just playing. No clear answer means NO. You say Ciao and move on. More on the topic of breaking up in Chapter 29.

Bottom Line

Continue dating your man until you know for sure that you can't date him any longer. Then breakup ASAP.

Chapter Twenty-Six

Getting Exclusive

Be courteous to all, but intimate with few, and let those few be well tried before you give them your confidence.

— George Washington

Remember your high school days, when guys and girls would agree to "go steady". Things aren't as simple anymore. There are no set rules that determine when a dating relationship should become exclusive. So how do you know when the time is right? Should you have a formal conversation to forge a binding agreement? You can if you want to. When you do, don't beat around the bush and try to use subtle hints and weird analogies to get your answer. That's just insecure, and can easily lead to misunderstanding. There's nothing wrong with telling a guy that you want your relationship to be exclusive. Just come out and say it. Make sure you get a straight answer. Demand it.

If you don't feel like having that conversation, for whatever reason, I think you still have the right to assume that your relationship is exclusive, and the obligation to treat it that way, under the following circumstances:

- 💜 If you've gone out on more than six dates, you obviously believe that this relationship has marriage potential. (If you don't you must have skipped the last chapter. Go back and read it, and move on.) That means you need to put 100% of your effort and attention into the relationship to make it work, which precludes you from dating anyone else. If he's still dating you, and you've been holding back like I told you to in chapter 22, you can assume that he's serious and committed too, unless you have evidence to the contrary. If you're seeing each other several times a week and speaking on the phone in between, you have no reason to think otherwise.

- 💜 If you've gone out less than six times but feel that you've developed a significant emotional connection, you should not date other people. For example, if you spent your first few dates talking for hours sharing your deepest feelings about everyone and everything dear to you, there's no reason for you to date anyone else. Just apply the 6+ date rule.

- 💜 If you've been sexually intimate you need to be exclusive. If anything, it's a health issue. I also don't see how you can date someone for marriage while having sex with someone else. It's just not kosher on so many levels. Obviously, he needs to be exclusive too. Any reason to believe he's not is grounds for immediate termination.

A research study of the dynamics of speed dating found that increasing option variety leads to chooser confusion. People are more likely to choose no one at all when faced with greater variety. They won't commit because of the fear of missing out on something better that might come along. This "fear of missing out" is based on reality. If you decide to commit to something, you might very well miss out on something better. If you buy the current model of your favorite automobile, you can be sure that a newer model will come out in less than a year. If you buy the latest ipad, you must be aware that a newer model with more features is probably just around the corner. Because of this, some people hold off on buying the current model. Some people never end up buying. Most people, however, decide to buy now because they need it now, regardless of what might happen in the future.

Cars and ipads are interesting, but let's face it, you can pretty easily trade in or sell them, or just buy a second one. Marriage is (supposed to be) forever. That's a heck of a lot scarier. If you let that fear get the better of you, you'll never get married. One way to conquer a fear is to overpower it with a stronger or more pressing desire or fear. Your desire to get married must overpower your fear of commitment. While you accept that there may be someone out there who might come closer to your vision of perfection, you also accept that you might never meet him and even if you do, he might reject you. All you can be certain of is the relationship that you have before you here and now. It's your job to try your best to make it work. As far as you're concerned, there is no one else to date except for the man whom you're dating now.

Chapter Twenty-Seven

Why Men Stay Single

I love to be alone. I never found the companion that was so companionable as solitude.

— Henry David Thoreau

You've probably known or dated more than your share of men who seem to have all the requirements necessary for marriage, but just aren't interested in tying the knot. Sure, some of these guys might just not be ready to marry YOU, but I think it's safe to say that many of them really aren't ready, or don't want, to marry, period. Age plays no factor in this. Men in their early 40's can be as unwilling or unready to marry as men in their early 20's. On the other hand, there are plenty of men who marry right out of college. In the "good old days", most men (and women) in their early 20's were married with a child or two. So what happened? Why do so many men choose to stay single?

Some men will attempt to claim that they just haven't met the "right one", but the overwhelming majority will admit (if

145

pressed) that there was at least one woman in their dating pasts that they could have married had they wanted to. So the question stands: Why do so many men choose to stay single?

The following reasons are in no particular order. Different ones apply to different men. You can choose the one(s) that fits best.

Freedom

There are many benefits to marriage. Freedom is not one of them. When you're single you go where you want when you want. You eat whatever, whenever. You are the sole master of your free time. You spend your money however you see fit. To use an old Seinfeld expression (albeit out of context), you are the master of your domain. Marriage changes all of that. Some guys just don't want to give up their freedom.

Excitement

Being a single guy is like going out on patrol in a combat zone every day not knowing what you will run into. Who knows what new woman you'll see and want to "get to know" better? Every subway ride or trip to Whole Foods holds the promise of new adventure. Every bar or party becomes a high stakes, adrenalin pumping challenge no less exciting than a twilight lion hunt on safari in Kenya. So what if you come up empty handed? There's always tomorrow.

Fantasy Quest

Every man has an image (or 2 or 3) of his ideal, fantasy babe. She often bears a remarkable resemblance to one of the latest Sports

Illustrated swimsuit models, or one of the many erotic stars that make regular appearances during late night private web browsing sessions. Since none of the real life women they meet match up to their fantasy partners, some men are willing to keep looking until they find one that does. And they keep looking, and looking. As long as they hold on to their dream of finding her, they will never be able to commit to a normal, attractive, flesh and blood woman. If they do commit, they might miss their opportunity to be with fantasy Barbie. So they keep looking.

Fear of Responsibility

With marriage comes responsibility. You don't need to be a super hero to understand that. With children comes HUGE responsibility. Now that's scary! Having a spouse these days doesn't really add much responsibility to a man's life other than fidelity (which unfortunately, for some men is too hard to handle) and visiting the in-laws (hopefully not too often). Having kids is another ballgame. A man might suddenly become the family's sole earner while expenses go through the roof. Then there are the late night or early morning wake ups, diaper changes, babysitting, diaper changes, exhausted (cranky) wives, diaper changes and more diaper changes. Some men just don't want any part of it and would rather sit around in their underwear drinking bear, watching football, dreaming of their fantasy woman, and enjoying a quiet, full night's sleep.

Never Really Grew Up

Marriage and children are for responsible adults who want to share and give. A good marriage depends on sharing and giving. Being a parent means giving 100% without expecting anything in return. Children are inherently selfish. Their primary concern is to get what they want when they want it. They spend their days eating, sleeping, and playing. They're not responsible for contributing anything. All they need to do is follow basic rules and instructions, and have fun. Some men never grow up. They remain perpetual children... and they like it that way.

So now you understand what you're up against. But don't despair. Most men do get married, eventually. You just have to get them when they're ready.

If you're in a relationship with one of these man-boys, it's probably only a matter of time before he gives you some lame excuse about how he's just not ready to commit right now, or something like that. When that happens, there's nothing you can do but say goodbye. Your only defense is to identify these guys before you've fallen for them hard, and it's too late.

Identifying them isn't easy. They seem perfect, right up until they break the news to you. Lucky for you, many of these guys actually do give you pretty clear hints about what their ultimate plan is. Some even tell you straight out. All you need to do is heed their words.

Dating Alert

When a guy says he's unavailable, believe him.

I once got a letter from a woman describing an almost fairytale romance with a man she was madly in love with. She wanted a serious long term relationship that would lead to marriage. Several times during the span of the relationship Prince Charming told her that he wasn't ready for a committed long term relationship. Instead of believing him and moving on, she tried to prove him wrong. She showered him with love and affection to make him realize just how wonderful she was and how he would never meet anyone who even comes close to her beauty, personality, and intelligence. How do you think the story ended?

When a guy says he's unavailable, believe him. Don't think that you possess the supernatural power to convert this guy into a believer. No amount of feminine seduction or persuasion will change this man's reality. He was nice enough to let you know that he's unavailable. The only thing you can do is pat him on the head, wipe his mouth with a napkin and, with the biggest smile you can muster, wish him well on his journey. Then run as fast as you can and find a guy who *is* ready to be in a relationship with you.

You might decide that you want this guy so badly that you're willing to wait as long as it takes for him to become ready. There are a few problems with that strategy.

- ♥ He might never be ready. Some guys never are.
- ♥ It might take him years to become ready. Are you seriously ready to spend years hoping that eventually this guy will marry you? I know women who did wait it out and ended up with their prize, but those years were full of frustration, doubt, insecurity, and anger. I know many more who wasted some of the best dating years of their lives waiting for guys who never were ready. When a 22 year old makes

that mistake, she's got plenty of time to recover. When a 35 year old woman wastes five years, the outlook is not as rosy.

You don't want to wait five years for a chance at marriage. You want to get married in the very near future. That's why you're reading this book. If this guy doesn't share your goal, he's not the right guy for you. You will find the right man. Trust yourself.

I'm happy to report that I recently heard of two instances (from the women involved) where the guys told them, after a few dates, that they were really not ready for a relationship, and the women said, "have a nice life" and fled. Hurray! They followed my rule and have since moved on to healthier and happier situations. You can and should...MUST...do the same. Trust your man. If he says he's unavailable, take him at his word... AND RUN!!!

Chapter Twenty-Eight

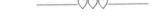

The Friend Zone

Between men and women there is no friendship possible. There is passion, enmity, worship, love, but no friendship.

— Oscar *Wilde*

Nobody wants to be trapped in the Friend Zone. Let me explain. When you really want to date someone, but instead end up being the one he calls to recount the details of his latest date, you are firmly entrenched in the Friend Zone. There's nothing wrong with being friends with a member of the opposite sex. In fact, it's great being able to get opinions and perspectives from the "other side". Many of my dearest friends have been women...when it was perfectly clear that we were not going to date each other. That's the key. You can have a deep, gratifying relationship with a member of the opposite sex as long as it's clear to both of you that you are just friends, and nothing more. You can even be physically attracted to your friend, despite what Harry (When Harry Met Sally) would postulate, as long as you honestly don't want to date her (yes, there are important things besides attraction). If one of you thinks otherwise, the relationship will be a tortuously frustrating one, primarily for the one longing for more. Trust me on this. You don't want to be friends with someone you have the hots for, watching them date just about everyone except you. It gets even worse when they start dating someone seriously.

Why would anyone voluntarily subject themselves to the pain of the Friend Zone? You either think that the target of your affection will eventually come around and realize that you are their true love, or you think that your friendship is actually a dating relationship.

Could they come around? We've all heard about that girl who played the part of the energizer bunny, and just kept going and going in the Friend Zone until, by some miracle, she actually emerged victorious and walked down the aisle with her "friend". It's true. It does happen, maybe .01% of the time. Are these the odds you'd like to stake your future on? You could be stuck in the hell of the Friend Zone for months, even years, without ever having anything to show for it other than a shattered heart and a huge block of wasted time and energy.

What about all the warmth, caring, connection, and nightly conversations that last for hours...doesn't that mean that you're dating? Well, let's see. Does he pay for you when you go to dinner or the movies? Does he call at least 24 hrs. in advance, to find out if you'd like to "hang out"? Does he look his best when he meets you? No = Friend Zone. The clearest sign that you're in the friend zone is if he talks about, or actually is, dating other women! You'd think that this is obvious, but in the Friend Zone, it's cloudy all the time.

How do you get out of the Friend Zone? You have an honest, grown up, totally open, heart to heart conversation with your friend, telling him exactly how you feel. Will this ruin your friendship? That's really up to you. If your friend tells you he's not romantically interested in you, you need to evaluate whether you can honestly accept your friend status and continue the friendship. If you decide you can (it is possible, but difficult) then do it. If you feel it's too difficult, then you must create distance. That doesn't mean you have to ignore and never speak to him again. You can remain friends, but not BFF's, the way you were before. You also need to evaluate whether you will be emotionally available to date other people while remaining friends. Many people say they can remain friends and date at the same time, but in truth they are still hoping for their friend to discover them romantically, and therefore, are not really open to other relationships. Friends with benefits? That's got disaster written all over it. Don't be foolish enough to think that your situation will be different.

On the bright side, when you have the big conversation, your friend might agree to explore a romantic relationship with you. It does happen! But don't wait too long to have that conversation. The longer you wait the deeper you'll sink into the Friend Zone abyss and the harder it will be to extricate yourself when your friend tells you he's engaged. Ouch!

SECTION FOUR

NAVIGATING YOUR RELATIONSHIP

Chapter Twenty-Nine

Lost in Translation

Think like a wise man but communicate in the language of the people.
— William Butler Yeats

Many relationships get derailed due to miscommunication. She said or did this, he said or did that, and the next thing you know you're sitting alone in your room scanning online profiles and wondering how you could have ever fallen for someone so unreasonable or insensitive. This can happen at any stage of a relationship, from first date through marriage. The setting and players are different, but the reason behind the inevitable fallout is the same.

Men and women speak different languages. They think and express their feelings in different ways. They have different needs and different expectations. If you're unaware of these differences, you'll constantly find yourself frustrated, confused, and hopelessly clueless. What you think is good will be bad, right will be wrong, complements will be insults, and humor will be mockery.

Let's go through some examples:

Does He Care?

Most women love getting flowers from their guy. It shows her that he thinks she's special. Guys don't really get the whole flower thing. That's because no straight guy ever wants to get flowers from anyone in any situation. In the guy's mind, buying flowers is just a waste of money. They just sit there and die in a few days anyway. Who needs 'em? The only way a guy will know to bring a gal flowers is if someone tells him to. If he's got sisters or female friends, or he saw his dad do it for his mom, he might get the message. If not, then unless you tell him how important it is to you, he probably won't figure it out on his own. If he doesn't, you must realize that it's not that he doesn't like you or care about you, it's just that he doesn't speak your language.

Is He Interested

Many women need to see that their man is interested in them, all the time. It doesn't matter where this need stems from. It's just there. Men don't always realize this. That's why they don't call several times a day just to hear your voice and they don't feel the need to go too far out of their way to accommodate you (unless of course the guy is still pursuing you, in which case he will do whatever it takes to win you over). You might interpret this behavior as lack of interest and caring, and assume that he'll make a rotten husband. In some cases you might be right, but in most, it's just a matter of speaking different languages. He does like you and care about you. He just doesn't express it the same way you do.

Is He Cheating

Just because a guy looks at other women or complements them doesn't mean he's interested in having an affair with them. I advise men not to complement, or even look at, another woman while in the presence of their woman. But he might slip up once and in a while. In fact, you might even try to trip him up to test him (you'd never do that). You might be walking along in Central Park with your guy on a sunny Sunday afternoon when you pass one of the Sports Illustrated swimsuit cover models.

"She's beautiful, isn't she?" you casually remark.

"Yeah", he innocently responds, taking your bait, banishing himself to the doghouse for an unknown time period, and opening himself up to an endless stream of questions, remarks, and comments that he'll find impossible to navigate.

The correct answer to your little test question should have been, "I didn't really notice" or "she's not really my type". Yes it's a lie, but it would have saved him from your hellish scorn. Why put him through all of that madness? So what if he acknowledges the beauty of another woman. That doesn't mean he doesn't think you're beautiful or that he's going to sleep with her.

Let's Talk

Sometimes a man just doesn't want to talk. He just wants to stare at a TV screen or immerse himself in something that is only interesting to the male species. If you try to talk to him about stuff that you think is interesting during those male moments, he won't hear you. Don't read anything into this. It doesn't mean anything about you or your relationship. You have two choices for remedying the situation. You can either do your own thing away from your guy or join him as a silent observer.

The examples I've listed here represent just a tiny sample of the potential opportunities for miscommunication between men and women. Although it's nearly impossible to never mess up, if you're sensitive to the language differences you'll have a much greater chance at a successful relationship.

Chapter Thirty

Is Full Disclosure Required in Dating and Relationships?

Seldom, very seldom, does complete truth belong to any human disclosure;
seldom can it happen that something is not a little disguised, or a little
mistaken.

— Jane Austen

If you're a publicly traded company there are strict laws that you must follow regarding full disclosure of relevant information. When you're in a relationship the rules of full disclosure aren't as clear. Am I saying that lying to a spouse or dating partner is ok? Well, it depends. What?!?! Yup, you heard me correctly. Let me elaborate.

There are different types of lies. There are what they call "white lies" or good lies, and bad, deceitful lies (black lies?). When you're a guest at someone's dinner table and your hostess asks if you liked the soup, it's obvious to all that even if you didn't, you lie and say you did. You might not want to be too enthusiastic about it though, because she might make you eat another serving.

When my wife asks me if she looks fat in what she's wearing, I probably should NEVER say yes even if it's the God honest truth. However, in my desire to make her feel good I might actually be harming her by letting her believe that she looks good when she really doesn't, and exposing her to the nasty comments of malicious scoffers that think they are guest hosts on the latest episode of Fashion Police. What I do is suggest something else that I think will look more flattering on her. I might say, "I think you look nice in this but I think that other outfit you wore last week looks much better on you." I've told her she looks nice and shown a sincere interest in her appearance, and I've given her some constructive advice that she will appreciate. I've triumphed where most men have failed.

Most guys couldn't care less if you criticize their fashion tastes. They welcome your suggestions. But there are other things that they do care about. Let's say your boyfriend is working as hard as he can but isn't making as much money as you think you'll need to live the kind of lifestyle you desire. If you fully disclose your feelings you will only succeed in making him feel like a loser. His financial situation won't improve, but I can assure you that your relationship will suffer. If you feel so strongly that you MUST disclose your feelings, speak to a close friend or a counselor. The only time you should tell him how you truly feel is when you're prepared to break up the relationship because of your financial worries. He has a right to know why you're dumping him. In any case, if you tell him you don't feel financially secure with him, you will ruin the relationship so, if you want it to continue, remaining silent is the right thing to do.

How much do you need to disclose about yourself, and your past? It depends on how long you are dating for. If you're on your first few dates, you really shouldn't have to disclose anything too personal unless, of course, you want to. When you feel that things are becoming serious then you must disclose things that will have a direct effect on your partner if the relationship progresses.

For example, if you're suffering from a serious medical condition that can severely affect your life or your ability to bear children, I believe that your partner has a right to know. But if you did things in your past that you are ashamed of and that you've totally given up, I don't think that you need to tell your partner. You've done your penance and made amends. You've got a clean slate. You don't need to tell your partner that you experimented with drugs in the past or that you once worked as an exotic dancer to pay your way through college, unless you're planning to continue taking drugs or stripping. It's none of your partner's business because it has no effect on him today or in the future. What happened in the past, stays in the past.

Now what if your partner directly asks you if you ever did such and such? Can you lie and say you didn't? Based on what I just said, the answer should be yes. However, there's another factor that comes into play. Why is this person asking you this specific question? If it's because he heard a rumor or has suspicions, then I think you might want to bring it into the open and come clean. Not because you have an ethical obligation to disclose everything. I believe that you don't. But you want to be with someone who appreciates you for who you are, not for who they want you to be. Everyone makes mistakes. You probably will make mistakes in the future. You both will. If your partner can't accept you, regardless of what you did in the past, then he is probably not the person you want to spend your life with. Making mistakes is part of life. So is moving on.

Basic rules to follow:

- ♥ White lies to avoid hurting someone are ok.
- ♥ Sensitive, constructive advice is even better.
- ♥ Full disclosure is only required when it affects the person you are disclosing to. If it doesn't, then it's your choice whether to disclose or not.

There are some things that you never want to bring up with your man, no matter how true they are or how strongly you feel about telling them to him. I know you think he can handle it. After all, he puts on such a macho facade, he can take anything you can dish out. Well, here's a little secret: men are taught to be strong and to suppress their feelings, but they're really quite sensitive and fragile deep down inside, particularly in the following areas:

Money

Most men need to feel that they are providing for their family. Even though times have changed since daddy brought home the sole paycheck and mommy stayed home to raise the kids and run the household, that image of the man being the bread winner is still ingrained in the minds of most men. Even today, in many families the old stereotype still holds true. If you tell your man, or lead him to believe, that you think he cannot support his family (or you) to the standard that you expect, you will crush him. You will shame him and make him feel so inadequate that he will either leave you to save face or become a shell of his former self (which won't be much fun). If you truly feel that he is incapable of providing, then you have two choices: 1) leave and find someone you think is capable or 2) make some money.

It's ok to encourage your man to strive to be better and reach his full potential. But you need to do it in a way that he will not view as an attack on his ability to provide. It's a delicate maneuver to make, but doable with the right sensitivity and awareness.

Sex

Men are competitive by nature. They strive to win, and hate to lose. Losing can make a man feel less of a "man". When you place the image in his mind of you having sex with another man, he feels like he's in a competition and you're the judge. All he can think about is how this other guy was better than him. It doesn't matter if this is totally false, and it doesn't matter how much you deny it and try to tell him that he is the best you've ever had. He thinks that you're lying to protect his ego (are you?). He feels insecure in his own ability. He feels like a loser. All he can see is this other guy giving you the time of your life. He has no choice but to leave you or forever cower in the shadow of the image of the sexual black belt who ruined you for all other men.

He knows you're not a virgin. He might even know who you were with. You don't need to talk about it. Keep your mouth shut. If he tries to bring it up, brush it off and move on to another subject. Make it clear that you've wiped away every memory you ever had of the other guy and don't remember a darnn thing. You got a virtual lobotomy. He'll be able to deal with that.

Machismo

There are certain things that a man is traditionally supposed to be able to do like: reading a roadmap, fixing stuff around the house, changing a tire, using tools, basic landscaping, navigating the Home Depot aisles. If you make him feel incapable of performing his male tasks, he'll feel like a loser and resent you for it. He knows that he can't do most of the crap guys are mythically supposed to do, but he doesn't want you to throw it in his face, especially in front of another man. It's ok for him to ask another man for help. It's not ok for you to do so in front of his face or behind his back. Let him try to get the job done himself. When he realizes he can't, he'll get someone else to do it. Just let him get to that realization on his own.

If you heed my words and avoid these three areas of discussion, you'll greatly increase your chances of relationship success and keep your man feeling happy and secure.

Chapter Thirty-One

Getting on the Same Page

What counts in making a happy marriage is not so much how compatible you are but how you deal with incompatibility.

— Leo Tolstoy.

If you're dating for marriage, being in a committed relationship is not your final objective. It is a process of exploration and discovery that, if successful, will lead to marriage. In many ways it is the best of all worlds. You no longer have to worry whether he'll call or if he likes you. You can enjoy love and intimacy, without legal or financial commitments. It's easy to get caught up in the romance and happiness of a relationship and forget that your primary objective is to determine whether your partner is suited to become your spouse.

You did some preliminary screening when you first started dating to make sure there were no glaring warning signs. You know you like, respect, and are attracted to the guy. He seems to be just what you're looking for, the answer to your I Do List. Now it's time to drill a little deeper to make sure that he's someone you can marry.

You don't have to agree on everything. You do have to agree on certain things. Only you can decide what those things are. You thought a lot about this when you created your I Do List. It's time to take out that list and start checking off items. You can decide at what point in the relationship to do this, but I can't see the benefit of waiting too long. The longer you wait the higher the risk of painful breakup. The only two items I'll insist you clarify, regardless of what else is on your list, are marriage and children.

You MUST make sure your partner shares your marriage objective. Not only does he have to want to get married, but he needs to want to do it within your timeframe. If you want to be married in a year and a half and he wants to in a decade and a half, you've got a *dealbreaker*. Too many women get hurt because they either didn't know or chose to ignore the answer they got. The only way to know if your partner shares your matrimonial goal and timeframe is to ask. Hinting doesn't count. You need to ask, straight up. When you get your answer you need to trust it, especially if it's not the answer you want to hear.

If you want children, you must make sure he does too. You should also clarify how many. If you don't want kids, or can't have them, you need to let him know too. Some men don't want children, for whatever reason. Some don't want more than one. Some may already have their quota from a previous marriage or relationship. If you're not on the same page regarding children, you probably should end the relationship.

You don't want to remain in a relationship, as great as it feels, if you know it's not leading to marriage. Letting go of someone you love and being alone are scary and painful, but I believe the alternative is worse. You might be lonely for a while, but then you'll meet someone wonderful who does want to marry, and find the kind of happiness you would have never experienced had you stayed in your previous relationship.

Chapter Thirty-Two

Makeup or Breakup

Before we can forgive one another, we have to understand one another.
— Emma Goldman

Relationships aren't always smooth sailing. Things go wrong. Mistakes are made. Tempers flare. You need to be able to discern between temporary malfunctions and permanent structural damage to know what to overlook and what to break up the relationship over.

Physical abuse of any kind is grounds for immediate breakup, period. I don't think I need to elaborate. Emotional abuse can be just as harmful as physical abuse, and often harder to recognize. It can destroy your self esteem and put your very self worth at risk. Make your partner aware that this is unacceptable and if there is no change head for the door" or something on those lines. If you feel that you're being abused in any form, tell your partner that his behavior is unacceptable, and seek professional assistance to help you diagnose the problem and deal with it. Most importantly, make sure you are safe from any further abuse.

Are there particular personality traits that you should beware of in your partner and consider breaking up over?

Dr John Gottman, one of the foremost marital researches, labeled the most detrimental emotional traits in a relationship, "The Four Horseman of the Apocalypse".

Criticism

When your partner verbally attacks your behaviors with the intent of proving you wrong and himself right. He typically does that by using generalizations such as "you always" or "you never".

Contempt

When your partner uses body language, tone of voice, or specific comments to hurt you or put you down. Eye rolling, name-calling, and sarcasm, directed at you, are all examples of contempt.

Defensiveness

When your partner tries to defer responsibility by attacking you. A classic example is "you think I did that, what about when you did that!"

Stonewalling

When your partner removes himself from the conversation in a way that may seem like he's trying to stay neutral but ends up showing disinterest and silently disconnecting, or just walking away during the conversation.

I don't know about you but these four horsemen sound mighty familiar to me. I admit, I've been guilty of most of them more than once (a lot more). I usually don't even realize I'm doing them. Most people don't, unless they're told. When you're faced with one, or all, of the four horsemen you should tell your partner how you feel in an open and honest, but non aggressive, way. You can say, "I felt really hurt when you rolled your eyes when I tried to make a point. Could you please try not to do that?" See how he responds. If he expresses regret and starts making tangible changes to his behavior, you're in good shape. But if he continues in his horseman-like ways, it's time to consider moving on. By the way, make sure you're not being a horseman either.

Anger

Anger is a normal, healthy emotion. When it rages out of control or becomes aggressive in nature, it becomes problematic or at worse, dangerous. If you feel physically threatened by your partner's anger you should end the relationship and suggest he get professional help immediately. If he gets the help he needs and overcomes his anger problem, you can reconsider. If you're not physically threatened by his anger, you need to decide whether it's something you're willing to live with. If you ask me, I wouldn't want to be with someone who had major anger management issues.

Cheating

- Contributed by Dr. Janice D. Bennett, PH.D.,
(www.DoctorLoveCoach.com)

Trust is the most important element in a successful relationship. What do you do when you find out the man you're in a relationship with cheated?

There are various definitions of what exactly constitutes cheating in a relationship. Most men define it as engaging in sexual contact with someone other than your partner. You might have a broader definition. It doesn't really matter how you define it. What matters is that you no longer trust your partner.

Cheating and breaches of trust in marriages have been in the news for years. President Bill Clinton and Senator John Edwards were married men when they "cheated," and their respective wives took different paths in response to their infidelity. Hillary Clinton stayed in the marriage, but demanded full transparency in Bill's actions, along with intensive couples' therapy. She ultimately forgave him. Elizabeth Edwards took a different path. Her sense of betrayal and anger prevented her from working on rebuilding trust, forgiving her husband, and staying in the marriage.

These examples demonstrate the choices you can make should you discover that your partner cheated on you. If you decide to make-up, then it should be after having serious conversations to clarify your expectations regarding the nature of your relationship and the responsibilities that go along with it. Determine if you are playmates, companions, or life partners. Discuss commitment and transparency and what it means to each of you. These conversations might best be had with the help of an objective third party, such as a couples therapist or relationship coach. Don't just jump back in. Take your time to see if you can re-build the love and trust. If your man shows remorse about what he's done and demonstrates that he's serious about never cheating again, you can choose to follow Hillary's path and continue to build your relationship. It's your choice.

If you feel your relationship has been irrevocably broken because of his breach of trust, then tell him that and move on. Without the enduring qualities of trust, honesty, and integrity, the relationship really doesn't have what it needs to endure. Staying in a relationship without feeling trust can corrode your happiness and well-being.

Knowing yourself and what you can and can't handle in your life, and your relationship, is the most important factor in your decision. Remember, your goal is to have a happy and healthy relationship with a man who you can trust. If you can achieve that goal with your present partner, great. If not, you'll find someone with whom you can.

Chapter Thirty-Three

Breaking Up the Right Way

Be kind whenever possible. It is always possible.

— Dalai Lama

"Breaking up is hard to do" is an understatement. But as terrible as it is, breaking up is a part of dating and relationships that everyone experiences on one end or the other, usually both, so it's important to know how to do the deed in the best and most sensitive way possible. When you've made your decision based on all the right reasons, here are some general tips to follow:

Don't drag it out.

As hard as you think breaking up will be, it will be even harder and more painful if you drag the relationship on and then break up. If you think there is a real chance of making it work then by all means take some more time to see it through. But if you've already made your final decision, DO NOT continue with the relationship. If you do you are just wasting his time, letting him become more attached to you, and preventing him from moving on and finding true love.

He will probably be furious at you for doing it, and rightfully so. Don't let it come to that. When you know it's not going to work, let him know ASAP.

Pick the right time and place.

Time to share a personal story. When I was studying in Jerusalem in 1991, I dated a woman for almost three months. Towards the end, while I was planning to propose, she was obviously planning to break up. In the meantime Saddam Hussein decided to shoot scud missiles at Israel and it became a stressful and demoralizing time as we stayed close to our sealed rooms and gas masks waiting for the sirens to warn us of the next attack. My girlfriend's family lived in a small village in a part of Israel deemed to be safe from attack, so she invited me to come out there to spend a couple of days away from the stress, and potential danger, of the city.

After a stressful bus ride to Tel Aviv (the main target of the Scuds) and then to her home, I made it there moments before the sirens blared. We donned our masks and entered the sealed room. The rest of my time there is a blur. The only thing I remember is that at some point during my stay she broke up with me and there was no way for me to leave until the next day (because of the wartime conditions). So in my heartbroken state I had no choice but to sit with her family in their sealed room, wearing my gas mask and feeling sick, and spending another night on their living room couch, only feet away from the woman who just broke my heart.

The point of this story is that when you do decide to break up, pick a time and place that is sensitive to the other person. I know I told you not to drag out the relationship, but a few days to spare the guy even more discomfort is not a bad thing. For example, if you've planned to go on a ski trip together in a couple of weeks, then you can break it off now, but if you're actually on the trip together, just wait until you get back home, especially if there are other people on the trip. Also, don't wait until the holidays or some special event to ruin someone's mood. Give him a little time to deal with things before having to face all of his friends and family.

I think the best, and maybe the only, way to gauge what the right time is for a breakup is to put yourself in the other person's shoes. Imagine how you would feel if you were broken up with at that particular time?

Give him a sense of closure.

Sometimes it's clear to both parties that a relationship is headed towards a breakup. In those cases, when the relationship finally does end, there's usually a sense of closure. Many times, however, the breakup comes as a complete shock to the other person. They are left dazed and confused, as if they were just hit by a speeding train and left lying on the tracks. From my experience, it's usually the guys who are the culprits in these situations (yes, I was guilty of it on several occasions). One day the guy seems all lovey dovey and then suddenly he's telling you it's over, have a nice life, I never want to see you again. Ok, that sounds a bit drastic but it just recently happened to a woman I was working with. Literally, out of nowhere!

Granted, breaking up is going to hurt the other person and there's no easy way to do it, but after it's done, you should at least try to give the person some sense of closure. What does that mean? Good question. It means different things to different people, but at a minimum you should have a face to face (if possible) conversation with the person and try to explain your feelings and reasons for discontinuing the relationship.

It's obvious that there are some things that you will never tell him because that would hurt him for no good reason, and that's fine. But there are certainly some things that you can tell him that will make him feel that the relationship was important to you, that he does mean something to you, and that he helped make you a better person in some way. It's still not gonna make him feel great or lessen his pain at that moment, but it will give him a sense of closure and when some time passes and he begins to heal, he'll view you in a positive, or at least neutral, light.

The worst thing you can do is break up with no explanation and then never speak to the guy again (assuming that he wants to speak to you). It might seem to make sense to you as the best way to help him forget about you and move on, but in the short run it's really hurtful and you deprive him of the closure that he needs to heal.

Space

Now that you've broken up and had a closure conversation, give the guy the space he needs to move on with his life. If you happen to frequent the same venues, find another place to hang for a while so that your ex doesn't have to see you and feel the pain over and over again, especially if you've already started dating someone else. I can still remember the pain of being on the other end of a failed relationship and having to see my ex on a regular basis. It's really painful. Give him a chance to heal.

Move on with your life.

You made the decision to break up and did the deed. You had the closure conversation. You are done. So why are you still calling him to chat or going out for coffee together? I know, you'd love to be friends with him because you really like him (just not as a spouse), but realize that he probably still has feelings for you. By continuing to interact with him in a close personal manner you are stirring up his feelings for you and possibly impeding him from wholeheartedly dating other people.

If you like him enough to really try again and make a serious relationship work, then give it your best shot and make it happen. Otherwise, please follow the words of Gloria Gaynor and "go on now go, walk out the door, don't turn around now, for you're not welcome anymore." Move on with your life and let your ex move on too.

What if you're the one who got cut loose? It really sucks. It's miserable. You feel sick. You either can't eat or you binge out on chocolate and ice cream. You just want to curl up into the fetal position, listen to the love songs only station, and cry your heart out. Need I continue? You've been there before. You thought this time would be different, but it wasn't, and here you are again.

I know how hard this can be. I really feel your pain because I've been there before many times. One of the things I did to try and pull myself out of my state of post breakup despair was to try and focus on all the things that were wrong about my ex and the relationship. It's funny how you can be miserable in a relationship but once the relationship is over, you suddenly remember only the good things about it. What about all the horrible shit your partner put you through? Oh, you don't remember that. Everything was perfect, and now it's all gone.

The ability to forget the bad is actually a blessing. As a rabbi of mine once said, "the greatest gift that God gave to humanity is the ability to forget." Without that ability we would be paralyzed by our recollections of every bad thing that ever happened to us. We would constantly be overwhelmed by grief over the loss of loved ones. Every trauma we ever experienced would be alive and fresh in our minds as if it had just occurred. We would simply not be able to function.

But in the case of a breakup, I want you to remember. I want you to make a supreme effort to remember all the things that weren't right about the relationship not so that you can hate your ex, but so that you can pick yourself up and move on with your life.

What if your ex and your relationship were perfect? Maybe it seemed perfect to you but it obviously wasn't perfect to him. If it was he'd still be with you. Do you really want to be with a man who doesn't think you are the one and only woman for him? Do you want to be with someone who doesn't think you are the best thing to ever walk into his life? Trust me, you don't. So as difficult as it is, and I know it is, you need to find the strength to be thankful for getting the chance to find a man who will love and cherish you like you deserve.

Even if you follow my advice you will still go through a grieving process similar to the one experienced after losing a loved one. You'll navigate through an array of emotions including sadness, denial, anger, self pity, despair, loneliness, and remorse. You might try to get back together with him, call him, stalk him, curse yourself for ever letting him get close to you, or conjure up fantasies of revenge. I don't recommend doing any of these, but it's your grieving process so I can't stop you.

There's only one thing that I can promise you to make you feel better. You will forget about him. In Jewish tradition the period of mourning for a parent is one year. From personal experience I can tell you that after that year the intensity of sadness diminishes. I can't tell you exactly how long it will take you to "get over" your ex. For some it could be weeks, for others months, but I will promise you this. You will recover and when you do, you will be stronger and more ready than ever to meet your true Mr. Right.

Do whatever it takes and take as much time as you need to heal. Grieve as much as you need. Then get out there and continue your mission to find your Mr. Right with a vengeance. Don't let anything or anyone get in your way of finding love. When you do finally find him, which I've noticed often seems to happen after a bad breakup, you will forget all about that *shmo* and focus all of your energy on your newfound happiness.

Chapter Thirty-Four

Long Distance Relationships

It is easy to be brave from a safe distance.

— Aesop

Online dating makes meeting men in faraway places easy. But is it wise to enter into a long distance relationship? The answer to this often asked question is as usual: it depends. The fact that he lives thousands of miles away from you is not a deal breaker per se. The successful long distance relationships I've seen all shared some common elements.

The most important prerequisite to long distance success is seeing each other in person. Chemistry is arguably the most important factor in a successful relationship. As good as your photos or video cams are, they are not the same as seeing someone face to face, in person. I can't explain it scientifically, but you know what I'm saying is true from your own experience. You don't want to waste a lot of time building an amazing online relationship, only to have it fizzle when you finally meet in person and discover that the chemistry is missing. To avoid this unfortunate situation, you should insist on a face to face meeting as soon as possible. By the way, this is true for any exclusively online relationship, regardless of where he lives. Unless you're just looking for a mindless cyber-flirtation, or you're a glutton for punishment, you must make sure to meet the man on the other end of those emails and pokes.

If a man is serious about you and about getting into a relationship, he will travel to meet you. If you want to be nice, and he lives really far, you can meet him halfway. But in general, you should not travel to see a man for the first time, unless you just happen to be going to his hometown on business. If he's really that busy with work, he should buy you a round trip ticket to come to him.

I've said this before and I'll say it again until you accept it. When a man is interested in a woman he will do whatever it takes to see her. That includes traveling thousands of miles, expending enormous financial resources, and even putting his life at risk. If he's not willing to make the effort to travel to you or bring you to him, he's not interested in you enough to make it worth your while.

There are lots of men who use online dating as a way to flirt without having to act. Most of these men are either married, in relationships, or not interested in getting serious. They are the ones who will say they want to see you but will never seem to have the time or ability to do so. They'll be traveling in Africa for months with no way of communicating, or they'll be stuck on a secret work project unable to travel or to even take a day off to see you if you come to them. You need to be able to recognize these scoundrels and avoid them like the plague.

If he's not willing to make the effort to travel to you or bring you to him, he's not interested in you enough to make it worth your while.

Once you've met in person and you're both interested, then by all means, you're free to carry on a long distance relationship, on one condition: You need to define a time limit for the long distance aspect of the relationship. A long distance relationship should be a temporary condition that exists only until the long distance aspect of it can be removed. Unless one of you is at some point planning to move to the other's city, there's really no point in getting involved. Who makes the move is not important. If you're open to it, then you should continue with the relationship. But be honest with yourself. You don't want to end up, months down the road, having to break up because you just can't make the move.

Finally, the only way to make any relationship work, especially one that is long distance, is to build momentum by communicating often. Your level of communication needs to make up for your lack of personal contact. Small talk once or twice a week just won't cut it. The relationship will fizzle and die in no time. You need meaningful communication by phone and email to build on that chemistry you already know you have from your personal meeting. The more you communicate the greater your desire to see one and other will grow until you just won't be able to be apart any longer.

Three elements to a successful long distance relationship:

- ❤ In person meeting ASAP.
- ❤ Defined time frame.
- ❤ Consistent and meaningful communication

Chapter Thirty-Five

A Word About Advice

Advice is seldom welcome, and those who need it the most, like it the least.
— Lord Chesterfield

When you need advice about something you ask someone who has been successful in whatever it is you're asking about. If you want to know how to get a job, you don't ask someone who's unemployed. If you want to know how to get rich, you don't ask someone who's broke. So why do so many singles get their relationship advice from other singles? It just doesn't make sense. Here you are trying to figure out how to build a successful relationship and you're asking advice from people who can't seem to do it themselves. You might say that you don't have to be in a successful relationship to understand the dynamics of one. Possible, but unlikely. Successful relationships are a direct result of hard work, compromise, and selfless giving. If you are in one, or have been in one before that ended due to circumstances beyond your control, you understand what I'm saying. I really don't care how many degrees you have and how much research you've done. If you haven't experienced it yourself, you can never truly understand.

If you just want to know how to attract men, you can definitely ask single friends. If you want to know what relationships and marriage are all about, ask someone who's in a committed relationship or marriage. When you're dating for marriage, getting serious dating and relationship advice from singles, be they friends or coaches, is just crazy.

Limit the amount of people you seek advice from to a maximum of one or two. You know that saying about too many cooks in the kitchen? Too much advice can be confusing. Sometimes talking about the same issues too much simply inflates them into something bigger than they are. When you find the people whose advice you connect with, direct your questions and issues exclusively to them.

Chapter Thirty-Six

Practice Makes Perfect?

Man plans and God laughs.

— Old Yiddish Saying

If you want to make sure you are matrimonially compatible with your partner, should you live together first to find out? Putting all religious sensitivities aside, if you believe the latest scientific research, the answer is no. The research concludes that couples that live together prior to engagement have lower quality marital relationships and are more likely to divorce than couples who waited. Without a socially recognized and binding symbol of commitment, people are less likely to put in the extra effort often required to make a marriage work. Why struggle and compromise when you can walk away stigma free? These days broken engagements are common enough to make me feel that the bond of holy matrimony is the only thing that's going to make a person stop and really think about how to fix their relationship.

Deciding to marry someone is a leap of faith. You'll never know if your partner is 100% right for you no matter how much time you spend together. You won't know even after you're married because getting to know someone is a process that just keeps on going. New situations arise that reveal new aspects of a person you would have otherwise never known. You can literally waste your prime years playing house trying to figure out what kind of husband and father this man is going to turn out as, or you can make a decision based on the important things you already have learned about him and play it out for real.

What more do you think you're going to learn about your partner by living with him? How he squeezes his toothpaste every day? Whether he likes doing household chores? What he's like when he comes home after a crappy day at work? Seriously, what information are you gaining that has any relevance to creating and sustaining a healthy marriage? Nada. What you will do is end up finding a ton of trivial flaws which will turn you off, make you abandon ship, and leave you swimming back home, alone.

There are practical reasons why a couple might want to move in prior to marriage. Sharing expenses is a huge one. Wanting to be together as much as possible is another. But if you can make it to the altar while remaining independent dwellers, I believe that you will add an aspect of newness and excitement to your relationship which you will otherwise miss out on.

You might disagree, and that's fine. You have every right to give it a shot and find out for yourself. If you're in your early twenties, no biggie if you have to wait a half dozen years to figure things out. But if you're in your thirties and above and are serious about getting married, you need to stop playing games and get serious ASAP. If you decide you must live together, set a strict time limit and stick to it. You'll never know for sure how your man will be as a husband, so go with the research and take that leap of faith.

Chapter Thirty-Seven

You're Engaged. Set the Date.

Things do not happen. Things are made to happen.

— John F. Kennedy

The right time to get engaged is when you and your partner both independently decide to take that big leap of faith and commit to marriage. I can't tell you when to make that decision. You'll know it when you're ready. Once you do get engaged, I think there is a time limit to how long the engagement period should last: as long as it takes to plan the wedding. That shouldn't take longer than a few months. Why you would want to be engaged for a moment longer than you have to? You've already decided to marry. Do so as quickly as possible and move on to the next stage of your life together.

The first thing to do after celebrating your engagement with family and friends is to set a date for the wedding. If either of you are unwilling to set a date, the culprit is not ready for marriage. If you're the one who isn't ready, you shouldn't have accepted his proposal in the first place. You need to seriously reevaluate your priorities or your relationship. One of them is off. If you really do want to get married, then you should break up with your partner because you're obviously not ready to marry HIM and probably never will be. If you don't want to get married period, you should do this guy a favor and cut him loose so he can find a woman who does (which shouldn't be too difficult).

If your partner is the one who refuses to set a date, you can give him a month or two to calm down and recover his senses. If after that time he still can't do it, you should end it and move on. Whatever's holding him back now will still be there no matter how long you give him. It's sad and unfortunate because you came so close, but it'll be even sadder if you're still engaged to him a year or two later.

Getting engaged means that you're getting married. That's why the classic proposal is, "Will you marry me" not "Will you be my fiancé". Engagement is a temporary arrangement, not a permanent status. I run into so many people who are engaged for years. That's their status. Some folks are single, some are married, and they're engaged. Do they have any marriage plans? No, but that's fine because they're engaged and that's good enough for them. Most of those engaged couples without dates end up eventually breaking up.

Bottom Line

If your final objective is being a fiancé, enjoy the ring and keep dreaming. But if you want to be married, set a date or get out.

Chapter Thirty-Eight

Limbo Land

Happiness is like those palaces in fairy tales whose gates are guarded by dragons: we must fight in order to conquer it.

— Alexandre Dumas

The time between getting engaged and getting married can be the best of times or the worst of times. It's really up to you to decide which one it'll be. You want your wedding day to be perfect. You've been planning it since you were a young girl. You know exactly how you want everything to look. You know exactly where you want it held. You've planned every single detail in your mind from flowers, to photos, to the color of the cocktail napkins. It's your special day, and no one better mess with it.

Everyone wants to see you happy, especially your fiancé, but life doesn't always play out the way you want it to. When things don't go exactly as you envisioned, how are you going to handle it? Are you going to keep things in perspective and realize that as important as your wedding day might be, it's still only one day in your life and your goal is to be happily married for the next seventy years (25,550 days)? Or are you going to raise hell, stomp your feet, and throw a terrible two's temper tantrum until you get things your way?

Let me introduce you to another player in your wedding day fantasy who will be making a surprise appearance and be staying for a long time. Her name is Mother-in-Law. She's the woman who wiped your future husband's ass, tucked him in, and kissed him goodnight. She thinks her boy is God's gift to mankind and is not quite certain whether you're up to the task of taking care of him. She's also been planning her little boy's wedding for a long time. If you and she happen to have the same wedding day vision, you've hit the jackpot and should celebrate. Chances are you don't. Now what?

If you or your folks are footing the wedding bill, you can politely tell mom-in-law that you appreciate her input and want her to be happy, but would prefer to do things according to your dream. If she's adamant in her position, consider compromising. Even though you've got the money to do as you please, she's got something over you that you can't compete with. She's your fiancé's mommy. That means she has the power to riddle him with guilt and make him feel like a piece of shit. I realize you can do that too, but that's not the point. He wants to keep mommy happy and off his case at all costs. That's part of the reason he's getting married in the first place. So if mommy is unhappy and future hubby is unhappy, who do you think is next on the list? Put your ego aside and do what it takes to make mother-in-law happy even if it means modifying your vision a bit. No, you don't have to do everything she says, but try to make her feel good even when you're saying no.

If your in-laws are footing the bill, you need to become a master of negotiation and try to get as much as you can while maintaining the peace. When you can't get everything you hoped for, just focus on the big picture. It's just one day in a lifetime.

Where is your beloved in all of this diplomatic maneuvering? Most men are happy to leave the wedding planning to you. The only details they really care about are venue, food, and music. The only criteria for food is that it's good and that there's lots of it. Same goes for music. The venue is usually determined by price. Most guys couldn't care less about the color of the tablecloths or variety of flowers.

Your fiancé just wants things to go smoothly. He is probably stressing out about the whole idea of spending the rest of his life with one woman. Nagging him about minor wedding details is only going to stress him out even more. Do you really want to do that? It's not that he doesn't love you or care about your wedding day. It's just that he doesn't care about colors and textures and styles. He's happy to let you run with the ball, as long as you stay within budget.

Yes, I said budget. If you and your man are paying for the wedding yourselves you need to weigh your wedding fantasy against the hard figures in your bank account. The last thing you want to do is to go into major debt that will haunt you throughout the early years of your marriage. It's stupid. If you have no money, elope. Don't go into debt, especially not credit card debt. Keep your eye on that big picture. Don't jeopardize your happy future together for a half day party.

When you're standing under that wedding canopy with the man you love, nothing else about that day will matter, unless you're petty enough to let it. Enjoy the fruit of your hard work. You found your Mr. Right. You're going to spend the rest of your life with him. That's the only thing that matters. Everything else is just part of the journey. You did it. Mazel Tov!

Final Words

I'm excited for you. I really believe that now that you're focused and have a plan, you will find your Mr. Right and go from I to I do. You might meet him right after you put down this book. But don't get discouraged if it takes a little, or a lot, longer. Remember, timing is everything. When it's the wrong time, Mr. Right becomes Mr. Wrong, or maybe Mr. Not Now. Don't worry, your time will come. When it does, you'll be ready to take advantage of it and turn a date into a relationship into a lifetime together.

I wish you all the blessings and good fortune in the world, and hope to dance at your wedding real soon.

There's More

No book can have all the answers or deal with every possible issue or scenario, so I created a website to continue addressing questions and issues related to your search for Mr. Right.

The address is: http://www.itoido.com

On the site you'll get access to articles, videos, and the chance to ask me questions and get answers.

So head over to www.itoido.com and subscribe for free!

Also by Arnie Singer

Goodbye, Mom: A Memoir of Prayer, Jewish Mourning, and Healing

How do you deal with a parent who is dying? How can you ease their passage from this world to the next? What prayers can you say to help them? What is the Jewish way of mourning and grieving? The answers to these questions and many more can be found within this book.

Goodbye, Mom: A Memoir of Prayer, Jewish Mourning and Healing, is a practical and spiritual guide embedded within the true story of the author's struggle to deal with his mother's passing. It is a moving story of hope and prayer, love and respect, mourning and grieving, and healing. Although the mourning customs are Jewish, the concepts of prayer, grieving, and healing discussed in the book are universal.

The Outsider's Guide to Orthodox Judaism

The Outsider's Guide to Orthodox Judaism is a handbook that explains the basic beliefs and practices of Orthodox Judaism in a clear and concise way. It is geared to anyone who is not Orthodox (or non Jewish) interested in learning more about their Orthodox coworkers, friends, and neighbors. It includes explanations of basic beliefs, rituals (like Sabbath and Kosher), lifestyle, lifecycle events, holidays, and more. Also included is a list of holidays and time-line of Jewish history.

Deep Waters: Insights into the Five Books of Moses and the Jewish Holidays

Deep and meaningful insights and explanations on the Torah and the Jewish Holidays.

Made in the USA
San Bernardino, CA
03 February 2013